MILLER'S Collecting the 19 60s

First published in Great Britain in 1999 by Miller's, an imprint
of Octopus Publishing Group Limited, 2–4 Heron Quays,
Docklands, London E14 4JP

Miller's is a registered trademark of Octopus Publishing Group Ltd

Executive Editor **Alison Starling**
Executive Art Editor **Vivienne Brar**
Project Editor **Elisabeth Faber**
Text Editor **Clare Peel**
Designers **Les Needham, Colin Goody**
Picture Research **Claire Gouldstone, Katherine Mesquita**
Production **Rachel Staveley**

Special photography by **Tim Ridley**, **Andy Johnson** and **Ian Booth**

The publisher would like to thank the following contributors:
Simon Andrews, post-war design specialist, Christie's South Kensington;
Henrietta Heald; Susan Hill; Sorrel Hirschberg, Victoria and Albert
Museum, London; Frankie Leibe; Stephen Maycock, Sotheby's,
London; Anita Phillips; Paul Rennie and all the dealers and galleries
who offered advice and assistance.

The publishers will be grateful for any information that will assist them
in keeping future editions up to date. Although all reasonable care has
been taken in the preparation of this book, neither the publishers nor the
compilers can accept any liability for any consequence arising from the
use thereof, or the information contained herein.

A CIP record for this book is available from the British Library

ISBN 1 84000 081 3
Set in Eurostile and Versailles
Produced by Toppan Printing Co., (HK) Ltd.
Printed and bound in China

MILLER'S Collecting the 19 60s

Madeleine Marsh

contents

Introduction   6

Chronology   10

homestyle   14

Italian Seating   16

Scandinavian and

German Seating   22

British Seating   26

French Seating   28

International Seating   30

Tables   32

Storage   36

40   Lighting

44   Technology

50   Kitchenware

54   Ceramics

60   Glass

66   Metalware

68   Textiles

72   Pictures and Posters

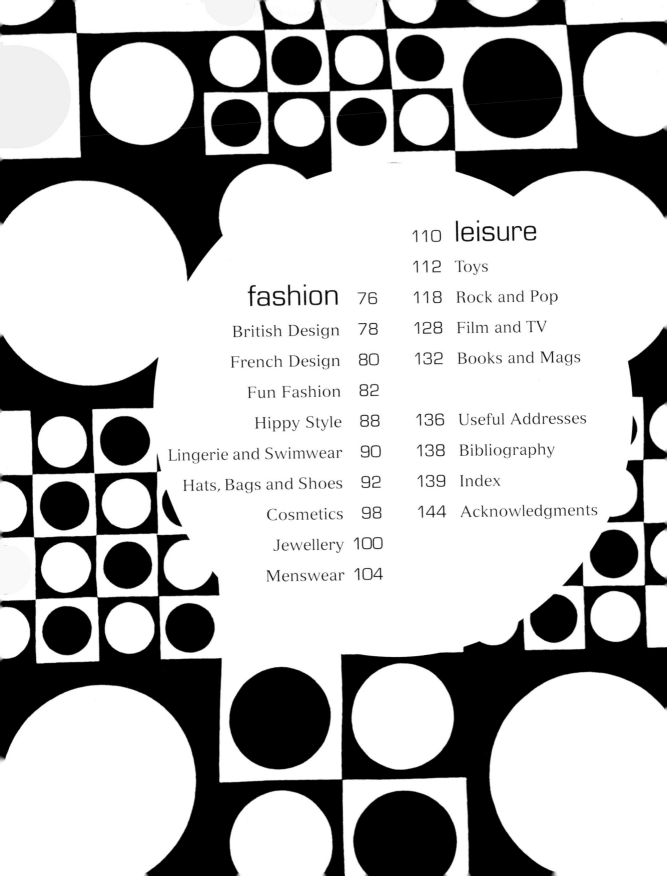

fashion 76

British Design 78

French Design 80

Fun Fashion 82

Hippy Style 88

Lingerie and Swimwear 90

Hats, Bags and Shoes 92

Cosmetics 98

Jewellery 100

Menswear 104

110 leisure

112 Toys

118 Rock and Pop

128 Film and TV

132 Books and Mags

136 Useful Addresses

138 Bibliography

139 Index

144 Acknowledgments

introduction

Born in the sixties, I was part of that generation who grew up hiding behind the sofa to watch *Dr Who*, and marvelling at the introduction of colour television. Memories of our family living room reflect the stylistic changes of the decade: the Scandinavian teak furniture, orange curtains and fluffy white rugs being replaced by Spanish chests, psychedelic textiles and Victorian carved-oak chairs.

My parents themselves, epitomized the social revolution that had taken place since World War II. Working in advertising (a profession that truly came into its own in the decade of throwaway culture), they both abandoned their working-class, provincial backgrounds for "swinging London". Saturdays were spent shopping in Soho for such delicacies as olive oil and French wine, followed by lunch at one of the new Italian trattorias, all white walls, pink table-cloths and raffia-covered bottles. Our whole family were enthusiastic members of the consumer society: I remember visits to Galt's for toys, Habitat and Elizabeth David's for kitchenware, and a peacock array of London clothes shops. My father favoured wide kipper ties, and striped and ruffled "Mr Fish" shirts. I remember my mother, dressed for a night out in a silver lurex dress and silver wig with scratchy glitter on her cheeks, and smelling of Ma Griffe perfume.

What with my parents' fashions and furnishings, my brother's records and Corgi cars, and my own Sindies, Trolls and Barbies, I could have photographed much of this book in our old family home, had we not been true to our disposable times and thrown almost everything away. It is not just what we keep that makes objects collectable, but what we discard. Thirty years on, sixties decorative arts are now appearing in antique shops to be purchased by a new generation of trend-setting shoppers.

This book celebrates the products of the 1960s in all their psychedelic colour. It begins by tripping into the sixties pad, looking at everything from blow-up chairs to lava lamps. The second section explores fashion: the rise of the mini-skirt, the trailing of the hippy kaftan and march of the kinky boot. The final part covers leisure, from the pleasures of children's toys, to the teenage explosion of rock and pop, to the substance-induced musings of the Underground press.

From Mary Quant to the Beatles, *Collecting the 1960s* explores the leading stylemakers of the decade through their creations. Objects illustrated come from across the world and reflect the diversity of an affluent culture. These objects are becoming increasingly collectable. At the top of the market, fine sixties design is now fetching four and five figure sums, however, much can still be found in flea markets and boot fairs. Every item shown is given a price range, reflecting current market values and what you might expect to pay for an object, not what you might sell it for to a dealer.

I would like to thank the dealers, collectors, auction house specialists and other experts who helped make this book possible. Anyone not old enough to have been at least a teenager in the 60s, can't help but feel they have missed out – but thanks to the contributors of this book, who shared their collections and knowledge – we can all enjoy the look, the style and the objects that made the sixties swing.

Mary Quant in August 1967 at the launch of her "Quant Afoot" range of boots. The boots were covered in clear plastic to keep the colours fresh and shiny.

Chronology

- French author Albert Camus dies, aged 46, in a car crash.
- John F. Kennedy becomes USA's youngest president.
- Biblical scrolls are discovered in the Judaean desert, Israel.
- Sharpeville massacre in Transvaal, South Africa – police kill 56 Africans.
- Alfred Hitchcock's film, *Psycho*, opens.
- First NHS hearing aids are issued in the UK.
- Congo becomes independent after 80 years of Belgian rule.
- In Ceylon, Mrs Surimairo Bandaranaike becomes world's first woman Prime Minister.
- Actor Clark Gable dies.
- Nigeria achieves independence from Britain.
- Inauguration of Royal Shakespeare Company in Britain.
- Harold Pinter, British playwright, publishes *The Caretaker*.
- Sylvia Plath, American poet, publishes *The Colossus*.

- Contraceptive pill, Conovid, goes on sale in Britain.
- Inauguration of John F Kennedy as President of the United States.
- BBC's *Children's Hour* dropped from broadcasting schedule.
- Anthropologist Dr Louis Leakey finds fossilized bones in Olduvai Gorge, Tanganyika, suggesting origins of a humanlike species date back to around a million years ago.
- Walt Disney's latest cartoon film, *101 Dalmatians*, opens.
- First man in space is 27-year-old Russian, Yuri Gagarin; he orbits the earth in a 108-minute flight.
- Malta gains independence.
- Fidel Castro, Cuban prime minister, repels American-backed invasion at The Bay of Pigs.
- Joseph Heller, American novelist, publishes *Catch 22*.
- Muriel Spark, British writer, publishes her novel *The Prime of Miss Jean Brodie*.

Hugh Heffner's Playboy Clubs opened in the '60s and the Bunny Girl became an icon of the new permissive society. Lighter: £25-35; Black ashtray £20-30; Orange ashtray £10-12; Pen £8-10

Famous for his pipe, Harold Wilson became leader of the Labour Party in 1963. He was known for his common touch and this cartoon is printed on a beer mat. £1-2

1962 1963 1964

- The Beatles pop group are rejected by Decca record company.
- Algeria achieves independence from France, following 132 years of French rule.
- Marilyn Monroe dies after taking an overdose of sleeping pills.
- Nelson Mandela is jailed for five years for incitement and for leaving South Africa illegally.
- Rudolf Nureyev, the Russian ballet dancer, makes his British debut.
- Alexander Solzhenitsyn, Russian writer, publishes *One Day in the Life of Ivan Denisovich*.
- Astronaut John Glenn becomes the first American to orbit the earth.
- The rock group Rolling Stones is formed.
- Director, David Lean, wins an Oscar for *Lawrence of Arabia*.
- Smallpox outbreak in Britain.

- The Beatles record their first LP, *Please Please Me*.
- Russian Lieutenant Valentina Tereshkova is the first woman in space.
- The Bond film, *From Russia with Love*, starring Sean Connery, is a great success.
- John Profumo, British Secretary of State, resigns from office over his affair with call girl Christine Keeler.
- Coronation of Pope Paul VI in Rome.
- American civil rights leader Martin Luther King delivers his famous "I have a dream" speech.
- Britain, America, and Russia sign the Moscow Treaty banning nuclear weapon tests.
- Beatlemania in Britain - more than a million copies of *She Loves You* sold.
- Assassination of John F. Kennedy in Dallas, Texas.
- Aldous Huxley, author of *Brave New World*, dies.
- Kenya achieves its independence.

- Mary Quant attacks Paris fashion as "out of date".
- Elizabeth Taylor marries Richard Burton.
- Jawaharlal Nehru, Indian prime minister, dies.
- Mods and Rockers clash on Clacton beach, England.
- Nelson Mandela is sentenced to life imprisonment for sabotage and conspiring to overthrow the South African government.
- Forth Road Bridge, Europe's longest bridge, is opened.
- Labour government comes to power after 13 years of Conservative rule; Harold Wilson is the new British Prime Minister.
- Bob Dylan records his song, *The Times They Are a-Changin'*.
- Roald Dahl, British writer, publishes *Charlie and the Chocolate Factory*.

US President J.F. Kennedy was assassinated in November 1963. £2700–2800

Beatles' spin-offs proliferated, such as this rare set of liquorice records. Set £220–250

Model, Jean Shrimpton, "the Shrimp" is featured on this pair of nylons. £6–8

1965 1966 1967

- Winston Churchill dies.

- Poet T S Eliot dies.

- Beatles member Ringo Starr marries Maureen Cox, a hairdresser from Liverpool.

- Malcolm X, black Moslem leader is murdered in Harlem, New York.

- American singer Nat King Cole dies.

- American comedian Stan Laurel dies.

- American and South Vietnamese warplanes attack North Vietnam.

- British actress Julie Andrews wins an Oscar for role in *Mary Poppins*.

- European protest against American involvement in Vietnam War grows.

- All four members of The Beatles are awarded MBEs.

- French architect Le Corbusier dies.

- Post Office tower, the highest building in Britain, opens; it is 62 metres high.

- Television ban on cigarette advertising.

- Mrs Indira Gandhi is elected as new Indian prime minister.

- Trial of Myra Hindley and Ian Brady at the Old Bailey, London, for the Moors murders; both are sentenced to life imprisonment.

- British novelist Evelyn Waugh dies.

- Bobby Moore captains England to beat Germany and win the World Cup.

- Chairman Mao launches his Cultural Revolution in China.

- Walt Disney dies.

- Elizabeth Taylor wins an Oscar for her role in *Who's Afraid of Virginia Woolf?*

- Successful soft landing on moon by *Luna*.

- Bechuanaland becomes Republic of Botswana.

- Aberfan avalanche disaster in Wales kills 144 including 116 children.

- British Government bans all trade with Rhodesia.

- Six-day war between Israeli and Arab states.

- Abortion is legalised in Britain.

- Actress Vivien Leigh dies.

- Latin American revolutionary Che Guevara is shot dead.

- First heart-transplant patient dies after 18 days.

- First microwave oven.

- Gabriel Garcia Marquez, Colombian novelist, publishes *One Hundred Years of Solitude*.

- Desmond Morris, British zoologist and writer, publishes *The Naked Ape*.

- Thurgood Marshall, American judge, becomes the first black member of the US Supreme Court.

- Kathrine Hepburn wins an Oscar for her role in *Guess Who's Coming to Dinner*.

- Joe Orton, British playwright and actor, publishes *What the Butler Saw*.

- American astronauts killed in fire during ground test at Cape Kennedy.

By the mid- 1960s, London was swinging and Carnaby Street was famous. Tom Salter's book provided a technicolour shop-by-shop guide to this centre of Pop fashion. £20–25

"World Cup Willie" was the winning England team's mascot and merchandise, such as this tiny Rolykin toy by Louis Marx appeared everywhere at the time. Boxed £30–35

1968 1969

- Martin Luther King is assassinated.
- Dry cleaners charge by the inch for mini-skirts.
- Richard Nixon is elected President of the United States.
- In London, Family Reform Bill lowers age of adulthood from 21 to 18.
- In the USA, Shirley Chisholm is the first woman to be elected to the House of Representatives.
- Russia invades Czechoslovakia.
- Barbra Streisand wins an Oscar for her role in *Funny Girl.*
- The Beatles form their own record company, Apple Corps, and release *Hey Jude* which sells over six million copies.
- Violent clashes between students and security police in Paris.
- Pope condemns all form of artificial birth control.

- Yassir Arafat becomes new PLO leader.
- In the UK, 1,600 female employees at a Ford car plant win equal pay with their male colleagues.
- Beatles musician John Lennon marries artist Yoko Ono.
- Golda Meir is elected Prime Minister of Israel.
- Human eggs are fertilized in test tubes for the first time.
- London-born gangster twins Ronald and Reginald Kray are jailed for murder.
- Concorde makes its maiden flight.
- Beatles musician Paul McCartney marries photographer Linda Eastman.
- Neil Armstrong is the first man to set foot on the moon.

Chronology

Surreal and psychedelic, The Magic Roundabout first appeared on British TV in 1965. This Pelham puppet is of Ermintrude the Cow Boxed £40-50

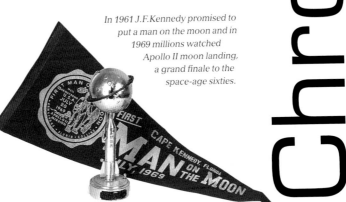

In 1961 J.F.Kennedy promised to put a man on the moon and in 1969 millions watched Apollo II moon landing, a grand finale to the space-age sixties.

Man on the Moon Cape Kennedy flag £15-20
John Glenn Destination Moon Money Bank £100-120

The 1960s was a decade of peace and love but also a time of rebellion against the Establishment. It was the decade that invented sexual freedom, youth culture and space travel. All of which were to have far-reaching influences on the look and design of everyday objects. "The Beatles really pricked the old fuddy-duddy balloon and the ripples touched and reshaped every aspect of our domestic lives," observed David, Marquess of Queensberry in 1968. Designers from Milan to Paris and New York had a fascination with looking at familiar objects in unfamiliar ways – making use of revolutionary materials and processes to develop new shapes and colours. This was the backdrop against which the prosaic reality of day-to-day living was revolutionized – pocket transistors, groovy telephones, dish-washer-safe ceramics, bean bags and televisions became commonplace in the home. The concept of lifestyle consumerism was born.

homestyle

italian seating

Italy dominated 1960s furniture design. The bean bag and the "Blow" chair, both Italian inventions, became icons of the new throwaway society and symbols of the trendy pad. Designers such as Joe Colombo made plastic seating acceptable in the smartest interiors, producing flexible furnishing systems for modern apartment living. Small "anti-design" groups revolted against the bourgeois notion of the traditional upholstered chair, creating fantasies intended to be objects of art as well as function. Italian design can fetch extremely high prices in the modern market, but condition is all important. The artificial materials that made such exciting shapes possible are prone to damage, and many pieces were intended to be disposable.

◄◄ The bean bag was apparently conceived by accident when some offcuts were thrown into a sack. Designed in 1968 by Piero Gatti, Cesare Paolini and Franco Teodoro for Zanotta, "il Sacco" epitomized the revolutionary spirit of the times. Light and portable, it was filled with polystyrene pellets that adapted to the body's shape. Bean bags were produced by many manufacturers, but beware of condition, as damp can cause the stuffing to swell and degrade.

£100–150

❦ The architect and Surrealist painter Roberto Matta (b.1911) was one of several artists commissioned by the Bologna company Gavina to create alternative furnishing designs. Named after Matta's wife, the "Malitte" seating system (1966–8) challenged the traditional concept of the three-piece suite. The five foam cushions offered different ways of sitting and could be moved about the room. When not in use, the shapes fitted together like a giant puzzle, to form a free-standing, abstract sculpture. "Malitte" was later produced by Knoll International from 1968 to 1974.

£3500–4000

➤ This sofa and chair designed by artist and film-maker Gaetano Pesce (b.1939) are part of the "UP" series of furniture that created a sensation at the 1969 Milan Fair. The polyurethane foam seats were compressed to one-tenth of their size and vacuum-packed into easily portable flat boxes. When unwrapped the brilliantly coloured shapes swelled to life, as if they were a type of instant art.

Chair £1200–1800   *Sofa* £2000–3000

➤ The Milanese firm Zanotta specialized in plastics, and the "Blow" chair (1967) by the design group Scolari, D'Urbino, Lomazzi and De Pas was its most famous product. This was the first mass-produced inflatable chair, made from transparent PVC (polyvinyl chloride) using a high-frequency welding process. Intended as fun furniture, it could be used indoors, outdoors or even in the swimming pool. The chair was prone to punctures and cigarette burns, and over time the plastic can turn an unpleasant nicotine yellow. Hence, collectors often prefer to buy unused stock. This model comes with box, foot pump and a tube of glue for mending blow-outs.

£400–450

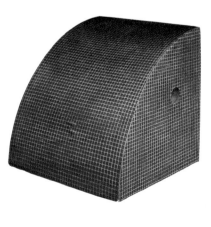

➤ "Wedge shape seating units in polyester foam are replacing the old fashioned pouffe," reported *House & Garden* in 1969. Gufram was among Italy's most radical design groups, and "Tourneraj" (1969) seems to defy sitting. But as you sink into the arched foam block, air escapes noisily from the holes, and the seat depresses, springing back as you stand up. Humour characterized much 1960s design, and Gufram went on to make a sofa based on Marilyn Monroe's lips.

£2000–2500

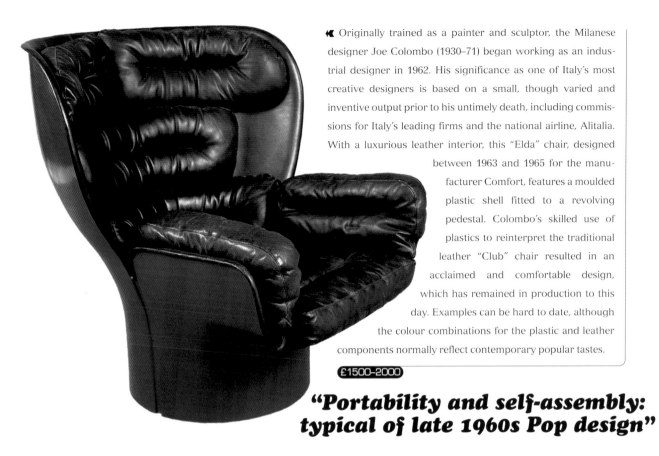

❮ Originally trained as a painter and sculptor, the Milanese designer Joe Colombo (1930–71) began working as an industrial designer in 1962. His significance as one of Italy's most creative designers is based on a small, though varied and inventive output prior to his untimely death, including commissions for Italy's leading firms and the national airline, Alitalia. With a luxurious leather interior, this "Elda" chair, designed between 1963 and 1965 for the manufacturer Comfort, features a moulded plastic shell fitted to a revolving pedestal. Colombo's skilled use of plastics to reinterpret the traditional leather "Club" chair resulted in an acclaimed and comfortable design, which has remained in production to this day. Examples can be hard to date, although the colour combinations for the plastic and leather components normally reflect contemporary popular tastes.

£1500–2000

"Portability and self-assembly: typical of late 1960s Pop design"

❯ Designed in 1969 for Flexiform-Prima, Joe Colombo's "Tube" chair comprised four plastic cylinders of diminishing size, each with a thin sheath of foam padding and a brightly coloured vinyl skin. The cylinders can be arranged or combined with additional "Tube" chairs to create a variety of seating options. When not in use the chair could be stacked concentrically in its own drawstring bag. The portability and self-assembly nature of this chair reflected the informal character of late 1960s Pop design. It was made in very limited quantities, and surviving examples are rare. The vinyl skin was prone to wear, and the drawstring bag was often misplaced, making examples in good, complete condition much sought after by museums and collectors.

£4000–5000

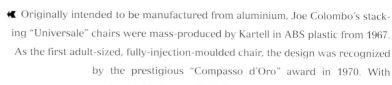

◀ Originally intended to be manufactured from aluminium, Joe Colombo's stacking "Universale" chairs were mass-produced by Kartell in ABS plastic from 1967. As the first adult-sized, fully-injection-moulded chair, the design was recognized by the prestigious "Compasso d'Oro" award in 1970. With detachable legs available in two heights, the design was easy to assemble. However, unlike examples made by other competitors, the chairs could only be stacked in units of three.

£80–150

▶ Mass-produced from 1969 by Castelli in clear acrylic and chromed steel, this "Plia" chair by Giancarlo Piretti (b.1940) was a popular reworking of the traditional folding campaign chair. Stylish, affordable and widely distributed, it was only 1in (2.5cm) deep when collapsed. The design won numerous accolades, including the German "Gute Form" award in 1973.

£25–50

◀ Unlike Joe Colombo's "Universale" chair, which required manual production-line assembly, the "Selene" stacking chair of 1969 by Vico Magistretti (b.1920) could be entirely moulded in one mechanical action. The commercial popularity of stacking or folding chairs in the 1960s was a result of increasingly small urban living spaces. Made by the Milanese company Artemide, "Selene" was available in many bright colours. Its fun, practical and economic qualities ensured it was one of Magistretti's most successful designs, and it was awarded the "Compasso d'Oro" award in 1970. In the early 1970s the chair was retailed in Britain by Terence Conran's Habitat stores.

£30–60

➤ Space-age styling and modern materials are evident in the fantasy form of this lounge chair. Called "Toy", this 1968 design by Rossi Molinary is made from a long rectangular sheet of folded translucent white plastic. The angle of the moulded chair recess is suggestive of a futuristic driving-seat, an impression enhanced by the crisp angular modern materials of the frame. A clear-plastic version of this chair was also produced.

£900–1200

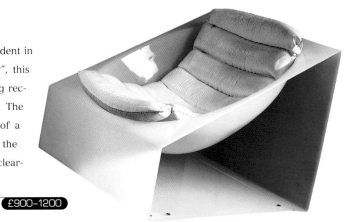

◀ The brothers Achille (b.1918) and Pier Giacomo Castiglione were prominent in Italian design from the late 1930s, their designs often Surrealist or sculptural in form. This elegant "San Luca" armchair (1960) combines luxurious materials with aerodynamic styling to create a striking form reminiscent of Italian Futurist sculpture. Assembled from only six main parts, the "San Luca" was produced in the 1960s by Gavina. Since 1990 it has been manufactured by Bernini.

£1500–2000

❦ Cut from a single block of foam, the two-part, wave-like form of this "Superonda" settee is an interactive design that can be arranged in a variety of shapes, with the emphasis on playfulness rather than practicality. Designed in 1966 by Archizoom (est.1966) and made in red, black or white vinyl, the "Superonda" has remained in production to this day, making it difficult to date specific examples accurately.

£400–800

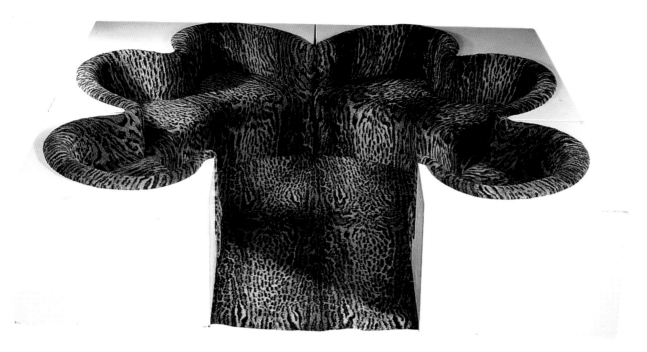

"It aimed to challenge notions of good taste and kitsch."

🔺 The "Safari" seating unit, designed by Archizoom and manufactured from 1968 by Poltronova, represented the revolution in living environments characterized by progressive late-1960s seating furniture. Comprising four interlocking fibreglass sections and dramatically upholstered in synthetic leopardskin, the "Safari" was architectural in scale and aimed to challenge notions of good taste and kitsch. The unit was highly priced and required a spacious interior – consequently few pieces were made, although with different fabrics.

£8000–12000

🔺 The radical Florentine design group Archizoom was responsible for some of the most progressive and challenging of all Italian seating. This uncomfortable-looking "Mies" chair and footstool were designed in 1969 and made by Poltronova. The combination of chromed steel and animal-hide cushions, together with a strict geometric styling, was intended by the designers as an ironic comment on the work of the Modernist designer and architect, Ludwig Mies van der Rohe (1886–1969). The flexible Pirelli rubber seat afforded a hint of comfort, and the underside of the footstool could be illuminated by a series of small light bulbs. The chair is acclaimed by collectors for its challenging, anti-design statement.

£3000–4000

scandinavian and german seating

Throughout the 1950s Scandinavian seating was characterized by natural materials and honest craftsmanship, and this tradition continued into the early 1960s with designers Grete Jalk and Hans Wegner. However, it was the work of Verner Panton that was set to revolutionize seating. From practical stacking chairs to free-form uphol-stered seating environments, Panton's combination of skill and imagination redirected the vocabulary of seating. In Finland, Eero Aarnio used plastics to create elegant chairs in space-age forms unseen in the previous decade. German seating in the 1960s was mainly represented by a crisp, rational approach, rooted in the traditions of the Bauhaus. This functional aesthetic can be seen in the chairs of Dieter Rams and Helmut Batzner. In contrast, the designers Luigi Colani and Peter Ghyczy both designed plastic chairs influenced by natural forms.

➤ This sensuous lounge chair by Grete Jalk (b.1920) is composed of two bolted ribbons of teak-faced plywood. Resulting from several years' research into the properties of plywood, it was produced by the Danish manufacturer Poul Jeppeson in 1963. Innovative, sturdy and eco-nomic, it could be made, claimed Jalk in nine minutes flat. "But," she noted sadly, "people are very conservative even in Denmark. They'll buy a chair with four legs, even three legs, but not many want one with no legs." Only c.300 of these chairs were manufactured, making good pieces highly sought after.

£4000–5000

◀ Upholstered in black leather and mounted on a chromed tubular-steel frame, this "Ox" chair of 1960 by Danish designer Hans Wegner (b.1914) has a powerful, masculine character. It is spacious, comfortable and, reputedly, a favourite of the designer. The broad curve to the top of the chair is character-istic of many of Wegner's chairs. The "Ox" has been in production since 1960, initially by Johannes Hansen and from 1992 by Erik Jorgensen.

£3000–3500

"the work of Verner Panton was set to revolutionize seating"

➤ Although the futuristic contours of this "Panton" stacking chair were first conceived by Danish designer Verner Panton (1926–1998) in 1959 and 1960, technical difficulties meant that it was not manufactured until 1968. A fluid, elegant design, the chair is durable and suited to mass production: it was produced first by Herman Miller, then by Swiss manufacturer Vitra. Marks on the underside of the chair will normally indicate the year of production. Examples manufactured between 1968 and 1970 utilized a different type of plastic and are most sought after by collectors. The upholstered metal chaise longue above is also a Panton design, manufactured by Fritz Hansen in 1973.

Chaise longue **£600–900**   *Chair* **£100–300**

◄ The zinc-wire "Cone" chair (near left), designed by Verner Panton in 1960, manipulates a material not normally associated with furniture production in an inventive and sculptural manner. A talented, eccentric designer, Panton once exhibited his new furniture designs by fixing them to the ceiling. "Cone" was part of a range of wire furniture he designed for the manufacturer Plus-Linje. Later examples are made by Fritz Hansen and will consequently differ in value. The high-back side-chair (far left) is an upholstered version of a dining-chair by influential Danish designer Arne Jacobsen (1902–72) for St Catherine's College, Oxford. This chair was made by Fritz Hansen after 1965 and was also produced as an armchair.

Side-chair **£150–300**   *Wire chair* **£700–1200**

➤ The late 1960s saw designers such as Eero Aarnio (b.1932) take Finland to the forefront of international design with the sophisticated use of synthetics to create modern, dramatic, space-age forms. This fibreglass "Pastille" rocking chair was designed between 1967 and 1968 and intended for both indoor and outdoor use. The flattened, spherical form with a shallow, scooped seat was surprisingly comfortable, and the chair won an A.I.D. award in 1968. Although the chair is durable, cracks or splits to the underside are common and difficult to repair. The chair was produced until 1980 by Asko, and thereafter by Adelta.

£400–500

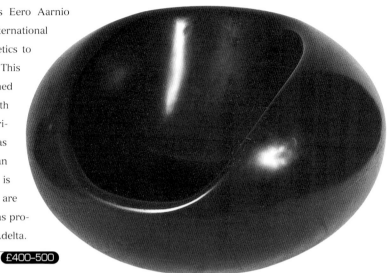

"one of the most iconic designs of the 1960s"

◄ One of the most iconic designs of the 1960s, Eero Aarnio's "Ball" chair of 1965 responded perfectly to the mood of the times with its crisp, white, globular form suggestive of space vehicles. Swivelling on a metal pedestal, the upholstered plastic shell afforded a great deal of comfort. The design was made familiar to the British public through its prominence in the television series *The Prisoner* and the film *The Italian Job*. Examples were also used in Mary Quant's boutique on Bond Street in 1968. Produced first by Asko, then from 1992 by Adelta, the chair features moulding details that allow fairly accurate dating. It should be remembered that the standard British door width is often too narrow for the "Ball" chair.

£1500–2500

➤ German designer Peter Ghyczy's fibreglass seat was intended for use both indoors and out. Appropriately called the "Garden Egg" chair, it was made from fibreglass and featured a hinged cover that created a watertight seal over the fabric upholstery. The production of versatile furniture for use in both the garden and the home illustrates the changing ideas of how domestic living space was to be used, and is in keeping with the growth of Green politics in Germany from the late 1960s. The chair has been in production with Reuter Produkts since 1968. Value is primarily determined by the colour combination.

£300–600

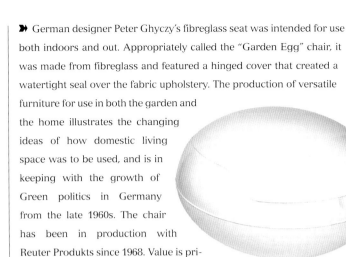

❦ This "Bofinger" stacking chair by German designer Helmut Batzner (b.1928) was designed in 1964 and presented at the 1966 Cologne Furniture Fair. Designed for mass production, it could be compression-moulded in five minutes and needed minimum finishing. In 1971 it was the subject of an exhibition, where noted artists made hand-made alterations to the chair.

£100–150

◄ A woven-wicker basket suspended from a metal frame, this lounge chair expresses the informality aspired to by many young consumers during the late 1960s. The manufacturer of this example is probably Swedish. Variations of this design were made in many European countries, and examples with metal cages hanging from springs can be found. The popularity of this design is shown by its use in contemporary magazines. For many, the hanging chair reflects the humour and imagination of the 1960s.

£250–400

british seating

By 1966 Britain seemed to the world to swing as never before. Paper, cardboard, flat-pack and modular became bywords for an exciting new direction in Pop furniture. A generation of young adults who had grown up under wartime rationing found liberation in disposable paper chairs printed with the patriotic colours of the Union Jack flag. Fuelled by the increasing numbers of students leaving home to study, modular or knock-down furniture was the solution to small city apartments. Terence Conran's furnishing store Habitat opened in 1964, offering a complete range of affordable products marketed at the discerning, stylish citizen. The revolution in British seating was not confined to the high street or to the art school. Robin Day's injection-moulded "Polyprop" chair combined practicality with economical materials to become one of the world's most durable and recognizable designs; the chair remains in production to this day.

◄ The "Polyprop" chair, designed by Robin Day (b.1915) in 1963, had a profound effect on the British furniture industry. For the first time lightweight polypropylene and new injection-moulding techniques were combined to mass-produce cheap seat shells. The shells were available in a variety of configurations and with a multitude of bases. A single moulding device could produce up to 4000 shells a week, and since 1963 over 14 million examples have been made.

£10–30

➤ "The young want instant homes as well as instant fashion," observed *House and Garden* magazine in 1968. Flat-packed paper chairs, were the ultimate instant furniture. Peter Murdoch made the first paperboard seats (1964–5), decorated with polka dots and intended for children. Fragile and disposable, they are hard to find today. The "Tab" chair for grown-ups shown above, designed in 1966 by David Bartlett, is even rarer and market value is very difficult to determine.

£1000+

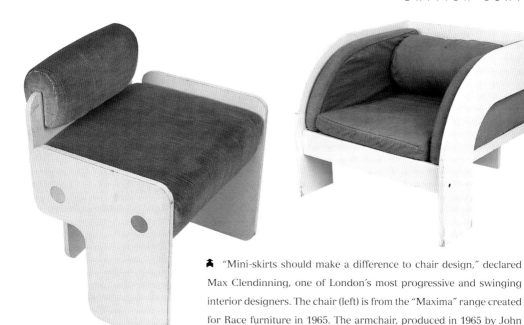

♣ "Mini-skirts should make a difference to chair design," declared Max Clendinning, one of London's most progressive and swinging interior designers. The chair (left) is from the "Maxima" range created for Race furniture in 1965. The armchair, produced in 1965 by John Wright and Jean Schofield, featured in the cult 1966 film *Blow Up*. Both knock-down designs, in white-painted plywood, these chairs are classic examples of British Pop furniture. However, their extreme rarity makes values difficult to determine and at present, high.

£1000+ *Each*

❦ This dining-chair, made from aluminium strips, was designed by William Plunkett for his company, William Plunkett Ltd (est. 1963). A former Army officer, Plunkett specialized in metal furniture: "I like the precision of the stuff," he claimed, "It doesn't move about like wood. And anyway I can't bear all that timber dust on my hands." Austere yet sensuous, Plunkett's furniture harks back to 1930s Modernist traditions and is increasingly collectable.

£200–250

◄◄ This chair was part of the highly successful "Tomotom" range of compressed paper furniture, designed in 1966 by Bernard Holdaway for Hull Traders Ltd, a company best known for its modern textiles. Furniture was available in seven colours and was low in price – chairs ranged from around £4 to £7 each. By 1969 over 100 designs were being produced, targeted at young home owners. Although this paper furniture is surprisingly durable, the cylindrical seats are not always comfortable.

£400–500

french seating

During the 1950s French furniture was epitomized by harsh, angular forms constructed of welded steel and plywood. By 1965 the mood had swung full circle as designers Olivier Mourgue and Pierre Paulin created a bold new language of soft, organic seating. Inspired by natural forms and using new types of foam and synthetic fabrics to conceal sinuous wood or metal frames, their chairs were rewarded with immediate international recognition. After the student riots in Paris in May 1968, there was a reaction within France to embrace these futuristic and playful designs, both in the home and the office. Within a few short years their chairs could be found in locations as diverse as the President's palace and airports in Paris.

❦ One of the most influential 1960s French designers, Olivier Mourgue (b.1939) studied interior design in Paris from 1954 until 1960. His most significant design is the "Djinn" series of 1965 (for manufacturer Airbourne), which was named after an Islamic mythological spirit that could alternate between human and animal form. The suite comprised lounge chairs, armchairs, a chaise longue and an ottoman, all with tubular-metal frames covered with a stretch-jersey fabric that gave a seamless organic appearance. When contrasted with the handcrafted wooden Danish furniture that dominated European interiors in the early 1960s, these chairs would have appeared highly radical. The bold, futuristic styling of these chairs was enhanced when they appeared in Stanley Kubrick's 1968 film *2001: A Space Odyssey* as the furnishings for the Space Hilton. The psychedelic fabric of the lounge chair below right increases its value.

Lounge chair £600–800

Chaise longue £800–1300

➠ Pierre Paulin's "Ribbon" chair was first exhibited at the 1965 Utrecht Furniture Fair, going into production in 1966 with Dutch manufacturer Artifort. A comfortable design, the chair earned Paulin (b.1927) an A.I.D. award in 1969. It is rare and can now be difficult to find examples in good original condition. After prolonged use, some examples have a tendency to sag slightly on the platform. Examples were also retailed with a psychedelic fabric, which would greatly enhance the value.

£1000–1800

"psychedelic fabric would enhance the value"

◀ Paulin was much influenced by organic forms, and nature is a consistent theme in his work. The form of this plastic dining-chair is suggestive of an opening flower bud, while the sinuous pedestal is rooted to the floor as if it were the shaft of a tree. This chair was designed in 1968 and manufactured by Boro. The actual number manufactured is unknown, but the few examples that have found their way onto the market suggest that production was limited. Variations of this chair were exhibited at the Paris Salon des Arts Ménagers in 1968.

£400–600

➠ The ribbon theme is again evident in this Pierre Paulin lounge chair. Variations with three parallel ribbons were also made. Paulin has become one of the most acclaimed contemporary French designers. Between 1968 and 1972 he helped remodel the public galleries of the Louvre, Paris, designing circular seating units. Between 1971 and 1985 he was commissioned by Presidents Pompidou and Mitterand to remodel and furnish rooms in the Elysée Palace, Paris. This "Ribbon" chair was made in large quantities and popularly used in the public spaces of French companies. Value is determined by the colour and condition of the fabric.

£200–400

international seating

The American furniture manufacturing giants Herman Miller and Knoll International dominated the international market during the 1960s. Chairs by Charles and Ray Eames, Harry Bertoia, Warren Platner and Eero Saarinen were mass-produced and distributed to both the residential and contract markets. The use of these progressive designs to furnish offices, town halls, museums and airports led to the widespread public acceptance of their modern styling. Other smaller firms responded to the popular taste by manufacturing affordable copies of inflatable chairs, giant floor cushions and bean bags. Occasionally, unique artist-designed chairs or ethnic and antique furniture enjoyed bursts of popularity, such as the "Peacock" chair, which was offered for sale in a 1971 Habitat catalogue as making "even the poorest hovel seem like an oriental throne room".

▶ American designer Warren Platner (b.1919) designed his range of nickel-plated wire furniture in 1966 for Knoll International. Of complex construction and with organic styling, the metal frame exploits the optical effects of light and shadow and thus shows the influence of Op Art. Some examples were also produced with a bronze wire frame.

£300–400

◄ The "Soft Pad" lounge chair was designed in 1969 by Charles Eames (1907–78) and his wife Ray Eames (1913–88). Intended for corporate use, it was made with a variety of bases and upholstery. Prices vary tremendously, with a premium paid for good leather upholstery. The pedestals also affect value, the most sought after being a low lounge-chair base or the swivel-and-tilt desk-chair base with castors. The chair is still made by the original American manufacturer, Herman Miller. Recent examples for the European market are made in Switzerland by Vitra. Unlicensed Italian copies exist.

£550–650

◀◀ In the 1960s there was tremendous experimentation with new synthetic materials. The improvement of production-line techniques ensured that objects could be economically mass-produced. This, together with the cheerful mood of the times, led to the acceptance of cheap, disposable fun furniture such as this inflatable armchair. Such chairs were mass-produced in many different countries, shapes and colours. The inflatable plastic cushion is a scarce example with printed decoration by American artist Peter Max. The psychedelic pattern is in keeping with the resurgence of interest in the late 1960s in the flowing curves of Art Nouveau.

Chair **£175–225**

Cushion **£35–40**

▲ Imported from the Far East, the handmade cane "Peacock" chair illustrated in the 1967 hippy interior on this album cover suggested a peaceful lifestyle liberated from synthetics, mass production, conformity and the Vietnam War. Glamorized by Brigitte Bardot, the chair sold into the 1970s.

Chair **£80–120**

Album **£25–30**

▲ With a torso length of nearly 7ft (230cm), this pink vinyl-and-fur settee with cushions would be hard to ignore. Created by the New York-based Belgian artist and set designer Nicola, only a handful of examples were custom-made between c.1968 and c.1970. The influence of Pop artists Claes Oldenburg and Tom Wesselmann is especially evident.

£4000–5000

31

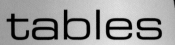

tables

Looking back at the 1960s, design historian Klaus-Jürgen Sembach mused that "tables of a normal height have become Cinderellas among furniture". Housing in the post-World War II period had undergone its own revolution – new homes were, on the whole, smaller than homes before the war, and their space less formally divided. Separate dining rooms were fast becoming a thing of the past, and new family units were growing used to living in flexible spaces with dining and living areas combined. Consequently, large, extending dining tables could no longer be sensibly accommodated in the home and gave way to smaller, folding, stacking versions. Reflecting the informality of new chair designs, tables also became smaller and lower; when lounging close to the floor in a bean bag, you needed to have your table at a corresponding height. Similarly, as the pattern of several large pieces of furniture in fixed positions became less common in interiors, people preferred small, light tables that could be moved around at will.

♣ Low coffee tables are among the most ubiquitous items of post-war furniture. Epitomizing the chic, leisured generation of the 1950s and 1960s, they evoke scenes of entertaining and relaxing at home. Tile-topped versions are fairly common and hint at the introduction of abstract art into interior decoration. Hand-painted tiles combined the artistic with the utilitarian, providing the perfect surface for hot drinks and those ever-popular fondue sets.

£200–300

♥ Two major concerns of the 1960s – leisure and space travel – are combined in this drinks table. Moulded compartments for storing bottles and a recessed area on the top to stop glasses from toppling are features that owe much to research into eating and working in zero gravity. This table, the little brother of the full-sized cocktail cabinet, was a "must-have" item for baby-boomers with more money and leisure time than ever before.

£300–500

➡ This multi-functional modular telephone seat and table in characteristic 1960s bright orange comes in four parts, which can be placed together to form one circular table, used separately or arranged in groups. Each segment of the ingenious design by Italian Rodolfo Bonetto is supported along its two straight edges, with the result that several segments can also be stacked into a shelf unit.

£200–400

"a production rate of one chair every four minutes"

◀ This plastic card table, designed by the German Helmut Batzner in 1966, was manufactured by Wilhelm Bofinger of Stüttgart, who also produced Batzner's "BA 1171" chair: the first one-piece moulded fibreglass chair. Both table and chair are in glass-fibre reinforced polyester, a material that derives its strength from the reinforcing fibres. The corner profile of the table legs mean that, like the chair, it is stackable. In a decade when mass-production of domestic products was paramount, Bofinger could boast a production rate of one chair every four minutes.

£100–250

➡ For Giotto Stoppino, making beautiful products affordable was the driving force in design. The benefits of working with plastics were their elasticity, functionality, strength and variety of form and colour that could be achieved. Like Kartell, for whom he designed these stacking tables in 1971, Stoppino believed in close collaboration between designer and manufacturer. Kartell began producing plastic household goods in 1954, turning to furniture in 1967. These stacking side-tables were made in white, orange, red, and black Cycolac, a form of ABS plastic widely used for its shiny finish.

£200–400

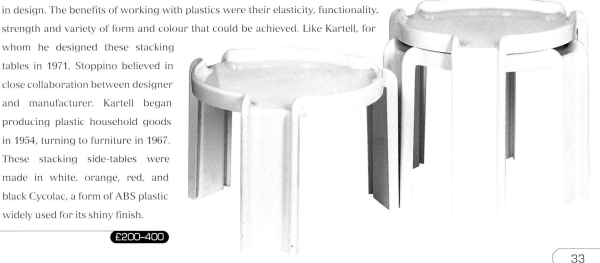

➤ The work of the designer Florence Knoll carries into the 1960s the styling of the 1950s, pioneered by Charles Eames (1907–78) and Eero Saarinen (1910–61), under whom she studied art and design in the 1930s. A pared-down Modernism combining functional shapes with quality materials characterizes her work for furniture manufacturer Hans Knoll, whom she married in 1946, taking over the directorship of the company after his death in 1955. This elliptical conference table available in expensive teak or rosewood is similar to tables by Charles and Ray Eames for Herman Miller from the 1950s. Both Knoll and Miller were hugely influential in establishing this type of post-war Modernism as the style for corporate interiors.

£700–800

"pared-down Modernism combining functional shapes with quality materials"

◀◀ Playfulness is apparent in much 1960s furniture, with many designers exploring scale, as with this table in the form of a giant spool. It was designed in 1966 by Bernard Holdaway for Hull Traders Ltd. The "tube" is actually made of compressed cardboard with a chipboard top and base, and painted in tough enamel. Although made from paper products the table is in fact extremely heavy and surprisingly durable for a Pop product. This fascination with looking at familiar objects in a different way is typical of the 1960s and the use of drugs by some, undoubtedly influenced the new shapes and colours seen in furniture.

£60–100

Using similar materials to designs by Florence Knoll and the Eames, this nest of wood-and-chrome tables takes their sleek, rectilinear Modernism out of the office into the home. Although associated with the period after World War II, nests of tables actually derive from early 19th-century nesting "quartetto" tables. During the 1960s, as in the 1840s when quartetto tables became popular, domestic living rooms became increasingly informal; nests of tables provided neat, space-saving solutions for rooms used for different activities and varying numbers of people.

£200–300

Flower power comes to the dining room in the guise of this plastic daisy-shaped table. There were many different flower-form-topped tables in the mid-1960s, the most famous being the "Tomotom" of 1966, which came with matching bucket seats that fitted snugly around each petal. This version relates most closely to a table designed by Pierre Paulin for Artifort c.1968 with four petals instead of six. Paulin's table has the same plastic laminate top on a narrow stem and splayed circular base. This type of pedestal base recalls Eero Saarinen's "Tulip" furniture of 1956, with one-piece moulded seats or circular table tops.

£500–700

Towards the end of the decade, disillusionment with the ultra-modern became discernable in design. Revivals of Art Nouveau and Art Deco styles appeared in popular music, graphics and fashion. This Biba table (c.1970) conveys the strong colours and geometry associated with both the Deco revival and with contemporary Op Art. The absence of similar items on the market has not yet permitted a price to be determined.

£1000+

storage

"Living space is rapidly shrinking, as houses are built with fewer and smaller rooms," worried *Ideal Home Magazine* in 1966; the article continued:

"... because of greater affluence and longer leisure hours families have more possissions than ever before. This causes an acute storage problem." Householders sought to resolve this problem with built-in and flexible storage systems. Habitat sold knockdown wall units that could be quickly knocked up in flats and bedsits. Plastic and paper storage boxes doubled up as tables. Major designers such as Joe Colombo (1930–71) experimented with space-saving forms that were multi-functional and moveable. However, not every storage solution was modern or plastic. A 1960s favourite was the Victorian wooden blanket box, bought for a snip from a junk shop, stripped of its varnish and painted with a psychedelic pattern.

♠ Florence Knoll's "Credenza" exemplifies the long, low seating and storage she designed for her own company, Knoll International, in the late 1950s and early 1960s. Widely imitated, Knoll's designs combine high-quality traditional and modern materials. Knoll was also successful as an interior designer, pioneering the open-plan office with integrated modular furniture systems that is so characteristic of the 1960s. Knoll International is also renowned for its reproductions of Modernist "classics" from the 1920s and 1930s by designers such as Ludwig Mies van der Rohe (1886–1969) and Marcel Breuer (1902–81).

£800–1000

◄ Designed c.1963 by Joe Colombo for Bernini, the "Combi Centre" was a multi-purpose storage unit. The top compartment has an internally lit Plexiglas band, surmounting box drawers and variously shaped containers, protected by sliding aluminium doors. It could serve as a bookcase, bar, table or even a tool chest, and came on casters so that it could be moved around the room. "Our century is characterised by dynamism," explained Colombo, "so it seemed indispensable to me to invent practical and useful elements, dynamic pieces of furniture."

£3000–5000

◀◀ Better known for his revolutionary forms for moulded plastic chairs and space-age lighting, Danish designer Verner Panton (1926–98) is also responsible for the "Barboy", produced from 1963. Cylindrical furniture that cannot be stored against the wall is characteristic of the Pop designers' emphasis on movement in interior design, underlined by the addition of castors to storage units. Maximum flexibility is provided by the undivided, swivelling drawers, which can be used to hold any small items.

£300–400

▶▶ The disposable and ephemeral character of Pop furniture is nowhere more explicit than in the paper and cardboard accessories made during the 1960s. The British paper record rack (left) is c.1967. The storage box is one of a series of prototypes by Anglo-American designer, Peter Gee. Made c.1966 it is unique and therefore impossible to value.

Record rack £250–350

◀◀ Everything the modern host needs to bring the kitchen to the party, the "Minikitchen" conceals a hob and refrigerator beneath the handy chopping board and storage tray. Designed by Joe Colombo for Boffi in 1963, this piece reflects the designer's preoccupation with reducing the clutter of domestic life and with the importance of flexibility in the contemporary interior. The design was awarded a medal at the 1964 Milan Triennale and included in the influential exhibition entitled "Italy – The New Domestic Landscape" held at New York's Museum of Modern Art in 1972.

£3000–4000

➤ Since the 1950s the influence of the expanding youth market had a profound effect on all areas of design. Taking the lead from popular culture, fashion was the most responsive to this trend, with new boutiques decorated in comic-book colours and space-age shapes to match the diverse and daring clothes they sold. This anatomically detailed torso hanger also reflects increasingly liberal attitudes towards sexuality, although it is not clear whether equally explicit male versions were made.

Hangers **£50–150** *Torso hanger* **£150–200**

➤ Joe Colombo's "Boby" trolley was originally intended for use in the drawing studio but its practicality and versatility ensured that it found its way into the kitchens, bathrooms and studies of the design-conscious. One of Colombo's best-known designs, the "Boby" trolley was manufactured by Bieffeplast from 1970 and available in red, yellow, black and white. Look out for the designer's signature, moulded in relief on the bottom shelf.

£200–300

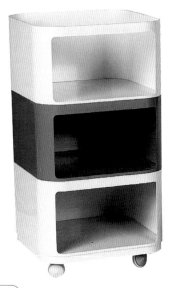

❮ Milan-based firm Kartell invested heavily in developing plastic manufacturing techniques and applying them to innovative, stylish designs for furniture, lighting and industrial products. These stacking modular storage units from 1967 are by Anna Castelli Ferrieri, one of the firm's top designers and a plastics technology expert. Her square units are part of a range of injection-moulded ABS plastic furniture she designed for Kartell in the late 1960s.

£200–300

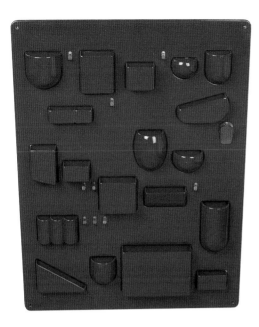

◀ Living systems designed for space travel inspired many designers to develop self-contained furniture units, like Joe Colombo's "Total Furnishing Unit". The "Wall-All", designed by Dorothea Maurer-Becher for Design M, Munich, in 1970, is a miniaturized version of these systems, where built-in storage and multiple functionality are the key. In this handy wall unit, each of the containers fits snugly into its own housing. The "Wall-All" is moulded in one piece from ABS plastic.

£300–400

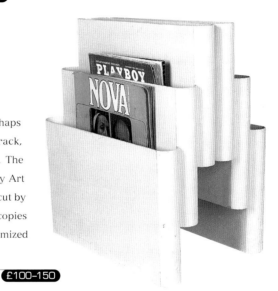

▶ Giotto Stoppino's architectural training is perhaps reflected in the character of this magazine rack, designed for Italian plastics giant Kartell in 1971. The curved ends of each section of the rack have a very Art Deco feel to them, although this revivalism is undercut by the use of ultra-modern ABS plastic. Look out for copies of *NOVA* magazine, which, launched in 1965, epitomized the mood and look of the swinging 1960s.

£100–150

◀ In a career spanning most of the 20th century the prolific French-born, American-based Raymond Loewy (1893–1986) designed everything from cars to cigarette packets, working for clients as diverse as Sears Roebuck, Gestetner and NASA. This "DF 2000" chest-of-drawers is part of a range of storage furniture designed in 1965 with Loewy's own firm, Compagnie de l'Esthetique Industrielle (CEI), and produced by Doubinski. The chest combines a metal frame with distinctive moulded plastic drawers and doors.

£800–1000

lighting

The 1960s was a period of huge variety in lighting, as designers sought to escape the glaring tyranny of the traditional overhead ceiling lamp. "There are spots, down lights, table and floor lamps that are sculpture, and modern materials like plastic, metal and paper", noted design writer Barbara Plumb in 1969. "Lighting is no longer just for illumination, but for atmosphere and in some instances psychological relief." The Italians were masters of flexible, fashionable lighting, creating stylish designs that adjusted to every practical need. High-street shops sold everything from cheap copies of the latest continental design classics to paisley-patterned, self-assembly paper lampshades. Designs were influenced by Pop fashions and space-age imagery, perhaps none more famously than the "Lava" lamp, a glowing symbol of the psychedelic generation. Growing interest in post-war design has stimulated demand for 1960s lighting, and while big-name pieces command the highest prices, stylish non-designer lighting is also becoming increasingly collectable.

It was not just the Italians who created innovative illumination. This white and silver "Moon light" is by Danish designer Verner Panton (b.1926). The aluminium slats could be adjusted in order to control brightness. From the mid-sixties, Panton created a whole range of dramatic, space-age lighting designs, including vast hanging chandeliers composed of chrome balls or irridescent, mother-of-pearl discs. His work was much imitated. This heavy plastic, yellow ceiling light is directly inspired by the Panton original and clanking copies of his chandeliers became, like the Peacock chair, one of the furnishing clichés of the hippy pad.

Moon light £250–350   *Yellow light* £70–80

These two lamps were created by Vico Magistretti (b.1920) for the Italian company Artemide. The "Eclisse" bedside light, far left, was designed in 1966. Resembling a spaceman's helmet, the aluminium light contains an inner shade that could be swivelled around to vary light levels and finally "eclipse" the bulb. The orange "Dalu" lamp, near left, with its organic, flowing lines, is made from moulded plastic and dates from 1969. Both of these lamps were produced in various colourways.

£60–65   *Each*

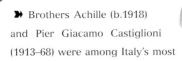

➤ Brothers Achille (b.1918) and Pier Giacamo Castiglioni (1913–68) were among Italy's most inventive lighting designers, and the "Arco" lamp, created by Flos in 1962, was perhaps their best-known product. Over 94in (240cm) high, the stainless-steel arc, springing from a rectangular marble base, was designed to hang over a dining table or seating area, providing an alternative to central lighting and added flexibility, since the height and angle of the light could be easily adjusted. This lamp appeared in fashionable homes across the world and was much imitated. This period copy is by the Italian firm Regiani and has a circular plastic stand. A Castiglioni original could be worth up to twice as much.

£300–350

◀ "The antiquated central overhead light, like a cyclopean Big Brother glaring down from the ceiling, should have had its day", commented *House and Garden* magazine, highlighting the contemporary fashion for a "diffused glow from lamps that double up as works of art". The "Falkland" light was designed by Bruno Munari (b.1907) for the Milanese company Danese in 1964. Released from their flat-pack, the white nylon-covered hoops extend to a length of 65in (165cm). The lamp originally retailed in Britain for £14 and 10s.

£350–450

▲ In 1959 Joe Colombo's father died, leaving Joe (1931–71) in charge of his electrical equipment firm. For 12 years, the Italian designer experimented with innovative lighting forms. Famous creations range from the clear perspex, C-shaped "Acrilica" lamp (1962) to "Alogena" (1970), the first halogen lamp for the domestic interior. This "Topo" ("Mouse") lamp dates from the same period. Made from stove-painted metal, the lamp could be attached to its base or clamped to a table. The shade rotates and the arm twists in every direction, reflecting Colombo's desire to create functional, versatile, mobile furnishing.

£150–250

41

➤ The "Lava" or "Bubble" lamp, near right, was designed by British engineer and prac-
tising naturist Edward Craven Walker. He created the prototype, a contraption made
out of a cocktail shaker and old tins, in a village pub shortly after World War II and over
the next 15 years perfected the secret recipe of oil and wax. Walker founded the
Crestworth company to market his new product, and in 1963 it was launched. Initially,
retailers were unenthusiastic: "They'd say, 'Take it away, it's disgusting!'" remembers
Walker. But as psychedelia took off, sales boomed and "Lava" lamps were made around
the world. The light became a hippy icon, providing the ideal ambience for taking
mind-expanding drugs, although Walker concludes: "If you have a 'Lava' lamp, you
don't need them." The example shown is British; the "Glitter" lamp, far right, is French.

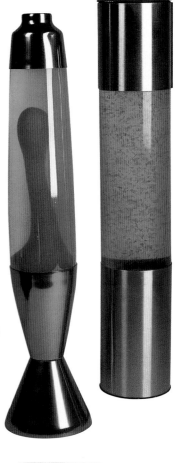

"Lava" lamp   **£60–70**

"Glitter" lamp   **£85–95**

"Take it away, it's disgusting!"

◀◀ The Italians were not the only ones to experiment with
plastic, adjustable, extending lighting. This little desk lamp
was made in Japan. The egg shape opens up to reveal a tele-
scopic light with a swivelling shade. Although it was made as
an inexpensive novelty item, its space-age styling makes this a
desirable piece today. Generally speaking, with non-designer
lighting, the more "hip" the design, the higher the price.

£45–65

➤ It was not just smart furnishing boutiques that sold colourful modern lights.
In 1968 the department chain British
Home Stores offered these cast-resin table
lamp bases, which came in amber, green or
blue, for 49s 11d (just under £2.50). Laminated
fabric shades could be purchased separately
in gold, orange, red, stone or turquoise.
While big-name designer lights from the
1960s can now fetch high prices, these mass-
market pieces are still very affordable.

Each   **£35–45**

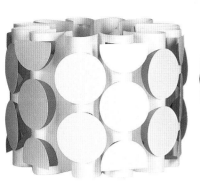
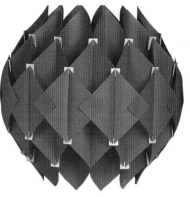

➤ Inexpensive, self-assembly lampshades were popular with young homeowners. Heavy plastic kits in bright colours and abstract shapes (such as the white and orange examples above) were imported from Denmark and cost around £3 to £4 each. Prices today depend on the Pop appeal of the design. Habitat sold paper shades for under £1 that could be put together in different forms: "Only 20 mins to make!" promised the packaging. For children's bedrooms, shades decorated with television characters, top right, were popular. A little less disposable is this 1960s Habitat table lamp (right), with perspex and acrylic elements designed for flat-packing and self-assembly.

White shade **£30–35** *Orange shade* **£20–25**

Magic Roundabout shade **£20–30** *Habitat lamp* **£65–75**

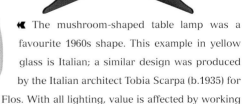

◀ The mushroom-shaped table lamp was a favourite 1960s shape. This example in yellow glass is Italian; a similar design was produced by the Italian architect Tobia Scarpa (b.1935) for Flos. With all lighting, value is affected by working order. To conform with safety regulations, all electric lamps should be earthed, and table and standard lamps should be connected to a 3-inch plug with a 3-amp fuse. Decorative condition is also important: check for chipped glass, scratched surfaces and any broken elements. The price ranges shown in this section reflect the fact that all of these lights are in good working condition.

£20–30

technology

In 1963, Labour leader Harold Wilson famously predicted "the white heat of a scientific revolution", and nowhere was this revolution hotter and whiter than in the field of domestic technology. British television ownership boomed from around 10 million in 1959 to over 18 million by the end of the decade, when an estimated 600 million viewers worldwide tuned in to watch the Apollo moon landing. With the introduction of colour television in the UK in 1967, the sets themselves became more colourful, with designs inspired by the space race. Previously families had gathered around wirelesses as big as cocktail cabinets; now teenagers tuned into pirate stations on the tiniest pocket transistors, while fun portable radios were shaped like anything from lipsticks to Coca-Cola bottles. Firms such as Braun offered a more minimalist and serious Modernism, but bright colours, shiny plastic and a fun approach are the keynotes of much collectable period technology, epitomized by the rose-red "Valentine" typewriter with its romantic name and case like a lady's handbag.

◀◀ The round, plastic television became one of the icons of the 1960s. British designer Arthur Bracegirdle broke the traditional square mould when, in 1969, he produced his famous "Keracolour" television, inspired by the shape of an astronaut's helmet. Also known as the "Sputnik", the orange "Videosphere" television above was designed in 1967 and produced by JVC from 1970. A small version with a chain could either rest on its stand or hang from its chain. The swinging design, with a smoked Plexiglas visor, came in orange, white and – rarer, and, therefore, more highly priced – tomato red. On the Grundig "Super Colour" television below left, one of the first remote-control models from the early 1970s, the globe has been stretched into an oblong. Both from cost and habit, however, most viewers still preferred a square television, and only 2250 of these sets were made in black, white and this golden-brown colour.

"Sputnik" £2000–2250
"Super Colour" £2500–3000

◄◄ ⬆ The influence of space travel skyrocketed throughout technological design. Conceived in the late 1960s, the Weltron "2004" AM/FM radio/cassette player above – also known as the "Space ball" – reflects the contemporary fashion for robotic plastic housings. Underneath the swivelling base is a giant rubber suction cup for increased stability, and this design (which features in the film *Boogie Nights*) could also be suspended from the ceiling. The speakers (Weltron "2003") were an optional extra, and it is unusual to find the set complete. Another rare UFO style radio/cassette player from the same period is the Philips "Vision 2000", shown left.

Philips **£1500–2000**   Weltron "2004" **£450–550**

"also known as the 'Space ball'…"

▶▶ The Weltron "2007" hi-fi (including turntable, cassette deck and AM/FM radio) was designed in 1966, available either as a table-top model or on a pedestal. Initially, it housed an 8-track tape system (invented by William Powell Lear of Lear jet fame), but from 1969 this was replaced by a cassette player. The turntable is protected by an anti-static pad decorated with an Op Art pattern by Aurea, Belgium. The portable Philips record player (type 22 GF 303/03 L), with a clear-blue plastic lid, was created by French designer Patrice Dupont in 1969. This model also comes with a red top. Such vintage equipment is popular with collectors and often purchased for reasons of style as much as listening pleasure.

Weltron **£1000–2000**

Philips **£100–150**

➤ "The aesthetic requirement of an industrial product is that it should be simple, carefully made, honest, balanced and unobtrusive," claimed Dieter Rams (b.1932), Germany's most important post-war industrial designer. He worked for Braun from 1955, where his creations such as this "AG-CSV 10" hi-fi (1964) were typified by austere yet elegant functionalism. Rams created a system of "product families", in which units could be added to and combined over time – a radical and rational antithesis to throwaway Pop culture.

£400–600

➤ Pop fashions filtered through into radio design, as advancing technology and mass-production methods permitted the creation of inexpensive, fun, plastic radios such as the "lipstick", "Batchelors tin" and "cup and saucer" shown right. Values depend on the novelty decorative appeal of the image rather than the quality of the sound.

Lipstick	£200–250
Batchelors tin	£100–120
Cup and saucer	£80–100

◀ This "Pop" plastic record player was designed by Mario Bellini in 1968 and manufactured by Minerva. Born in Italy in 1935, Bellini trained as an architect at the Milan Polytechnic and went on to design items as diverse as typewriters for Olivetti to furniture for Cassina. Italian industrial designers fought against low-cost Japanese goods and German high technology, with colourful style. Bellini once said: "The whole machine is beautiful, to make it a pleasure to have near you."

£25–45

➤ The transistor was invented by Bell Laboratories, USA, in 1948, paving the way for the creation in 1955 of the transistor radio. The first pocket-sized transistor (Sony's "TR63") was in 1957, and soon every teenager was tuning into a tiny portable. The miniature example above by the Standard Radio Corporation, Japan is extremely small, measuring only slightly more than a 50p piece. The "walkie-talkie-style" transistor shown right by the German firm, Telefunken, reflects the trend among designers of taking inspiration from technology and science-fiction.

Miniature **£200–250** *Telefunken* **£20–25**

◄ This black-and-cream "RL200" radio, manufactured by the British firm of Roberts, is also familiarly known as the "handbag" model. First released in February 1960, the radio sold for just over £14. Marketed as a style item, as well as a highly practical portable, it was available in an enticing range of coloured leather, most commonly red, blue, green, brown and black. Roberts also produced some rare novelty versions in ponyskin, leopard spots and jewel-encrusted suede. For the more opulent still, there was a model covered in real mink, and even a radio with a solid-gold case, retailing for a monumental £2000 guineas, not including the battery. Values for radios such as this are determined mainly by colour, condition and – most importantly – an eye-catching and attractive design. Collectors tend to prefer earlier transistors and a good dating trick is to check the timing scale. Pre-1963 models include small triangular civil defence marks indicating emergency radio frequencies for use in the event of a nuclear attack.

£25–45

❮❮ The "Grillo" (Cricket) telephone above was created by Marco Zanuso and Richard Sapper in 1965 and made by Italtel (the Italian National telephone service); it won a number of major design awards. This miniaturized fold-up model provides a dramatic contrast to the more traditional design of the British "Standard 700" series desk telephone – in use from 1959 until the late 1980s. However, the bright red colour lends this example its own Pop appeal.

Red phone **£20–25**   *"Grillo" phone* **£100–150**

➡ The "Valentine" typewriter, designed by Ettore Sottsass (b.1917) and Perry A. King and manufactured by the Milan company Olivetti, was launched on St Valentine's Day 1969. Sottsass described it as "an anti-machine machine". Breaking away from the grey and serious image of traditional office equipment, the bright red, moulded plastic portable typewriter slotted into a handbag-like carrying case. It was conceived as a domestic fashion accessory, created, claimed Sottsass "for use in any place except an office, so as not to remind one of monotonous working hours, but rather to keep amateur poets company on quiet Sundays in the country or to provide a highly coloured object on a table in a studio apartment".

£100–200

➤ "Appliances are instruments," stated Dieter Rams (b.1932), "not works of art. They fulfil a function, and design must serve that function. The goal it seems to me, is to help limit and reduce the chaos of the world about us." Designed by Rheinwold Weiss in 1961, the award-winning white desk fan, far right, epitomized the cool, scientific simplicity of Braun's products. The Braun fan, centre, is a 1971 version of the same design with only a one-, as opposed to a two-, speed setting. The model on the left is an unnamed plastic German copy of the Weiss original.

German copy **£20–25**   *Yellow fan* **£35–45**   *White fan* **£60–80**

➤ "We live in a throw-away economy," wrote the architectural historian Reyner Banham in *Industrial Design* (March 1960). This cardboard clock, designed by Paul Clark and produced by Perspective Designs Ltd, epitomized the new demand for instant gratification and is now highly collectable.

£200–250

➤ The mood of political protest that characterized the 1960s spilled over into its decorative artefacts. No student bedsit was complete without a poster of Che Guevara, and anti-establishment messages were emblazoned on everything from t-shirts to cushions. Dating from the late 1960s, this Chinese alarm clock, depicting Mao Tse Tung and his little *Red Book* from the Cultural Revolution, captures the spirit of the times.

£45–50

◄ The "Cifra 3" table clock was created by Italian designer Gino Valle in 1966, using a system he had devised for electronic signboards in stations and airports. The large numbers flip over on the cylinder and, as white on black, can be read from a distance. Made from moulded plastic, the clock proved a bestseller for its manufacturer, Solari & Co., and is viewed as a modern design classic, an icon of chic simplicity.

£100–150

kitchen-ware

The 1960s saw a food revolution as well as a social one. The Italian coffee bars of the 1950s were joined by trattorias, pizzerias and spaghetti houses. "Pasta has almost become the staple diet of Londoners... [who] are nonchalantly dextrous with a forkful of gleaming spaghetti," noted Len Deighton's *London Dossier* guidebook in 1967. If the straw-covered Chianti bottle became one symbol of changing eating habits, another was the red plastic ketchup bottle. By 1969 there were 460 Wimpy bars in the UK, and hamburgers became a family favourite. American-style convenience foods were popular in the new self-service supermarkets, while delicatessens introduced the British to the continental European delights of garlic and olive oil (previously available only from chemists for medicinal purposes). Kitchenware varied in style from the brown earthenware dishes and orange cast-iron casseroles bought from new stores such as Habitat to brightly coloured plastic and boldly patterned equipment that brought Pop fashion into the kitchen.

◄◄ While many designers were eager to experiment with plastics, others preferred to find new ways to work with traditional materials, such as glass and wood. This elegantly sculpted 1960s ice-bucket, for example, is made of teak. Its creator was the Danish designer Jens H. Quistgaard (b.1919), whose work was sold in the USA by Dansk International Design, a company that did much to promote modern Scandinavian domestic style to an international market.

£100–150

►► The popularity of influential British designer Mary Quant spread far beyond the fashion scene, and many trendy young things who bought her clothes also wanted the lifestyle to go with the youthful, lively "look" that she had identified as the hallmark of the age. This stainless-steel "Mary Quant" toaster, which is decorated with the designer's distinctive daisy motif, was one of a selection of fun, Pop-influenced designs manufactured by Morphy Richards and targeted at a young, fashion-conscious audience.

£40–45

◀◀ The influence of Italy made itself felt in the space-saving, stackable "Compact" tableware designed in 1964 by Massimo Vignella (b.1931) and Lella Vignella for ARPE. Made of melamine – a tough, lightweight plastic – the practical range was dominated by cylindrical forms and featured moulded handles. From 1969 "Compact" dinnerware was made in a spectrum of bold colours by Heller Designs.

£100–200

▶▶ "Entertaining in the kitchen has become as much a matter of course as buying clothes at Marks and Sparks," noted *House and Garden* magazine in 1964. "You can lessen labour by using oven-to-table ware: tough, fireproof casseroles and soufflé dishes... decorated delicately or gaily with flowers, or stripes or squiggles." Both British, the Pyrex casserole decorated with brightly coloured vegetables, top right, and the paisley saucepan set, bottom right, are typical of period kitchenware. Cheap and cheerful in their day, such items can still readily be found in flea markets and at car-boot fairs. The orange Le Creuset cast-iron casserole, centre right, was bought c.1962 from Mme Cadec's kitchenware shop in Soho. Mme Cadec, a redoubtable French woman, was among the first to import Le Creuset and other French kitchenware into Britain, paving the way for Elizabeth David's kitchen shop and Terence Conran's Habitat.

Top and Bottom **£12–15**

Middle **£20–25**

◀◀ The mauresque design, far left, called "Salome", was created by Ian Logan and manufactured by JRM Designs in 1967. It reflects the growing influence of Eastern-style and ethnic fashions. Op Art meets psychedelia in this set of six printed tinware placemats (maker unknown). The geometric compositions that dominated graphics in the early 1960s were later overtaken by more fluid, distorted Op Art patterns.

£100–120 *Salome (set)* £60–65 *Op Art (set)*

▶▶ These ceramic canisters are decorated with an interpretation of the "Carnaby daisy", which had its roots in the Mary Quant motif. Manufactured by Crown Devon (S. Fielding & Co. Ltd, Staffs, England) and painted in reds and oranges – the era's most popular colours – the jars were perfectly suited to the age of flower power. The lower-case typography recalls the lettering used by Conran for Habitat.

£8–12 *Each*

◀◀ "We all entertained in the kitchen, it was much more fun than a fuddy-duddy dining room," remembers one 1960s housewife. A small, but potent symbol of this growing informality was the replacement of the traditional cup and saucer by the mug. Both these mugs were made for *Private Eye*, the satirical magazine founded in 1961, which sold mugs such as these to help raise funds for their numerous and celebrated court cases. The Op Art example on the right is designed by Paul Clark. The mug on the left is inscribed with the words: "Grab, Probe & Grope". The children's mug is decorated with a scene from *The Magic Roundabout*, the surreal and psychedelic television series launched in 1965. The programme became a cult favourite among children and adults and Dougal and friends appeared on a host of merchandise.

Magic Roundabout mug £5–8 *Private Eye mugs* £80–120

❦ The growth of package holidays was pioneered by such entrepreneurs as Sir Freddie Laker, and the Continent became accessible to more people than ever before. Spain was the mecca of the masses, many of whom returned with souvenirs such as these below, which are collected by fans of kitsch.

Coasters (set) **£6–8**

Oil and Vinegar **£15–20**

🔺 The company Dodo Designs Ltd specialized in tinware. Their products both satirized and celebrated the Victorian era, giving a Pop twist to Britain's imperial heritage. Both of these "Best Tea" tins are based on Victorian prototypes and decorated with portraits of Boer War generals. The same spirit of eclectic revivalism was to be found in shops such as "Granny Takes a Trip" and "I Was Lord Kitchener's Valet", which sold vintage clothes alongside modern products, reflecting renewed interest in once-despised art and design from before World War I.

£50–60 Each

◀ 🔺 Television advertising came into its own in the 1960s. The Homepride men were conceived in 1964. These plastic spice jars (dating from the 1970s) grew out of television commercials featuring Fred and his team of flour-graders. In 1969 the company created its first plastic, Fred-shaped flour-sifter. Over 500,000 figures were sold in the UK, inspiring a wealth of Homepride merchandise and resulting in a collectors' club, the Friends of Fred. During World War II, powdered potato, known as "Pom", was a symbol of austerity; in 1967 Cadbury/Typhoo renamed it "Smash", and the Smash "Martians" became a television hit, inspiring promotional goods.

Smash "Martian" **£25–30** Homepride spice jars **£30–40**

ceramics

"The Beatles really pricked the old fuddy-duddy balloon and the ripples touched and reshaped every aspect of our domestic lives," observed ceramic designer David, Marquess of Queensberry, in 1968. Like everything else, ceramics were affected by the 1960s revolution, and, if one word can sum up the production of the decade, it has to be diversity. Tastes ranged from mass-produced commercial china to hand-thrown studio ware created by a new generation of craftsmen potters, whose work reflected their commitment to the alternative lifestyle. "Cylindrical and conical shapes are appearing everywhere", noted *House and Garden* magazine in 1964. Manufacturers experimented with new, geometric forms, and surface decoration reflected every passing fad and fancy, from multi-coloured Pop Art to black-and-white Victorian prints, to Oriental designs: "Distinctions of race, tradition and culture are becoming blurred," concluded Sir John Wedgwood. Leading names in 1960s ceramics include Midwinter, Poole, Portmeirion and Troika, and the best works of the period are now attracting a growing band of collectors.

➤ The 1960s saw the expansion of the Poole Pottery studio under design director, Robert Jefferson. With Guy Sydenham and Tony Morris, Jefferson experimented with new shapes, glazes and abstract decoration, resulting in the launch of the "Delphis" collection at Heals in 1963. This bold, hand-decorated ware successfully bridged the gap between commercial and studio pottery and is highly collectable today.

£75–100

❦ Troika was founded in 1963 by sculptor Lesley Illsley, potter Benny Sirota and architect Jan Thompson. Clay was prepared in a dough-mixer, and shapes devised to pack the kiln as fully as possible. Each handcrafted piece was conceived as a work of art, with moulding inspired by the local Cornish landscape, Paul Klee's abstract paintings and contemporary art. Although the ceramics establishment prophesied failure, Troika lasted 20 years, selling such items as this vase (designed by Alison Bridgen) and lamp through Heals, Liberty & Co. and leading design stores world-wide.

Lamp **£100–200** *Vase* **£100–120**

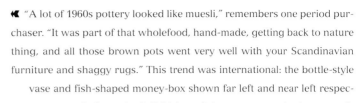

◄◄ "A lot of 1960s pottery looked like muesli," remembers one period purchaser. "It was part of that wholefood, hand-made, getting back to nature thing, and all those brown pots went very well with your Scandinavian furniture and shaggy rugs." This trend was international: the bottle-style vase and fish-shaped money-box shown far left and near left respectively are both British, and the square vase in the centre is by the Danish firm of Royal Copenhagen. A finely crafted piece, by a big-name factory, it is correspondingly more highly priced than the British items.

Bottle and "fish" (each) **£25–35**

Vase **£130–150**

▶▶ The bright orange colour and abstract style of these German vases – both of which are inscribed in German – are characteristic of 1960s decoration. While pieces by big-name factories such as Poole, Troika or Royal Copenhagen are already commanding high prices, anonymous pieces and those by lesser-known manufacturers can still be very affordable. Prices depend on the appeal of the design and the condition, so check for cracks, crazing and chips.

£15–25 *Each*

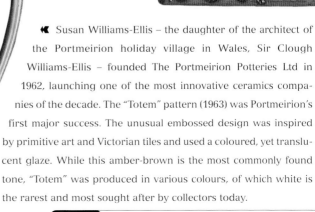

◄◄ Susan Williams-Ellis – the daughter of the architect of the Portmeirion holiday village in Wales, Sir Clough Williams-Ellis – founded The Portmeirion Potteries Ltd in 1962, launching one of the most innovative ceramics companies of the decade. The "Totem" pattern (1963) was Portmeirion's first major success. The unusual embossed design was inspired by primitive art and Victorian tiles and used a coloured, yet translucent glaze. While this amber-brown is the most commonly found tone, "Totem" was produced in various colours, of which white is the rarest and most sought after by collectors today.

£40–45

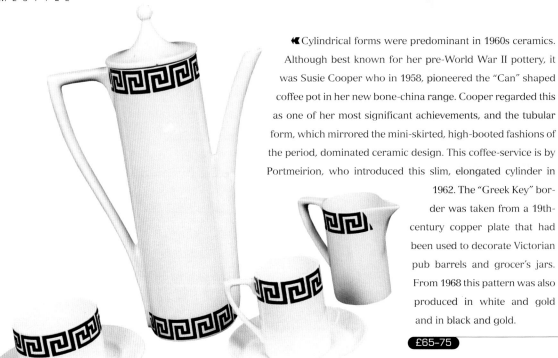

◄◄ Cylindrical forms were predominant in 1960s ceramics. Although best known for her pre-World War II pottery, it was Susie Cooper who in 1958, pioneered the "Can" shaped coffee pot in her new bone-china range. Cooper regarded this as one of her most significant achievements, and the tubular form, which mirrored the mini-skirted, high-booted fashions of the period, dominated ceramic design. This coffee-service is by Portmeirion, who introduced this slim, elongated cylinder in 1962. The "Greek Key" border was taken from a 19th-century copper plate that had been used to decorate Victorian pub barrels and grocer's jars. From 1968 this pattern was also produced in white and gold and in black and gold.

£65–75

➤➤ Abstract decoration flourished on ceramics. The Studiocraft planter right (c.1960–62) was made by Hornsea Pottery, which specialized in well-crafted, contemporary earthernware. "We make no traditional products and would now expect almost everything we produce to be accepted by the Council of Industrial Design," claimed John Clappison, principal Hornsea designer along with Martin Hunt and Philip Turner. The container by Crown Devon below features an Op Art pattern. A term coined c.1965 for a new form of abstraction using optical techniques to disrupt and fragment the vision. Op Art was pioneered by painters such as Bridget Riley and Victor Vasserelly and plundered by makers in every field of the commercial decorative arts.

Hornsea £40–50

Crown Devon £25–35

◀ In the 1950s Midwinter became one of Britain's leading makers of stylish tableware and in the 1960s the firm went from strength to strength. In 1962 David Queensberry introduced the "Fine" range, shown here decorated with Jessie Tait's "Sienna" pattern. Modern, cylindrical, straight-sided forms inspired by the historical precedent of the milk churn.

Cup and Jug **£5–7** Each
Coffee pot **£10–15**

▶▶ In addition to employing resident designers such as Jessie Tait, Roy Midwinter commissioned patterns from a range of fine and decorative artists. Best known for her textile designs for Heals, in 1964 Barbara Brown created the "Focus" pattern for Midwinter shown on these pieces. The best-selling design reflects Brown's interest in Op Art, balancing colours and geometrical shapes to create a three-dimensional pattern on a flat surface. The coffee pot is also by Brown and was manufactured by Johnson Bros.

Jug and bowl **£12–16** Coffee pot **£80–100**

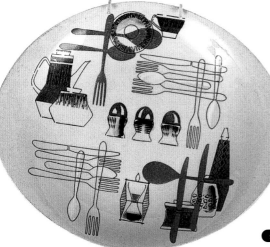

◀ This "Fiesta" plate was made in the early 1960s by Barker Bros, Royal Tudor Ware. Influenced by Enid Seeney's "Homemaker" pattern (1955), the dish illustrates the contemporary style in domestic tableware. However, it is not just the front that demonstrates modern fashions. Turn it over and the backstamp includes the words: "Dishwasher proof", reflecting the increasing popularity of labour-saving appliances.

£10–12

➤ Susan Williams-Ellis's first ceramic designs were made for the Portmeirion souvenir shop in the 1950s, when she commissioned Gray's Pottery to produce a series of lustre wares decorated with Victorian prints. In 1960 she and her husband took over Gray's and in 1961 they acquired Kirkhams, a tumbledown ceramics factory, with attics concealing a wealth of 19th-century copperplates and moulds that the new Portmeirion Potteries transformed into the latest Carnaby style. This Portmeirion "Comfortable Corsets" coffee set is decorated with images from a Victorian underwear catalogue. The cup and saucer are from Portmeirion's "Chemist Print" range inspired by labels from 19th-century medicines. The photographic plate is part of a series called "Where Did You Get that Hat?" and is inscribed "Chaumette, Paris – Made in England."

Coffee set **£250–350** *Plate* **£40–50**

Cup and saucer **£40–50**

❦ This plate and mug, by British designer Paul Clark, reflect two top Pop Art emblems. American artist Jasper Johns became famous for his target painting in the 1950s, and by the 1960s, the target motif was seen on everything from t-shirts to record covers. The Union Jack flag, a symbol of swinging Britain on this mug from "I was Lord Kitchener's Valet", was given a boost in popularity when England won the World Cup in 1966.

£80–100 *Each*

◀ This "Beefeater" salt-and-pepper set and Noah's ark money-box are by Carlton Ware. Established in 1890, the Stoke-on-Trent company was taken over by Arthur Wood & Sons in 1967 and became well known for its witty, tongue-in-cheek designs. However, beware since a number of Carlton Ware fakes exist that were made from original moulds that went missing when the factory sold its premises in 1989.

Beefeater set **£25–30**

Money-box **£35–45**

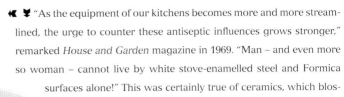

❮❮ ❦ "As the equipment of our kitchens becomes more and more stream-lined, the urge to counter these antiseptic influences grows stronger," remarked *House and Garden* magazine in 1969. "Man – and even more so woman – cannot live by white stove-enamelled steel and Formica surfaces alone!" This was certainly true of ceramics, which blossomed with big flowers and bright colours. These plates were made by Washington Pottery, Staffordshire. The oil and vinegar set, measuring jug and jam pot are by Lord Nelson Pottery. The pattern – called "Gaytime" – features bold, colourful graphics that are typical of the style that predominated from the late 1960s into the 1970s.

Plates (each) **£4–6** Jam pot **£8–10** Jug **£20–25**

Oil & vinegar set **£12–15**

"ceramics blossomed with big flowers and bright colours"

❮❮ This handsome ceramic lemonade set, decorated with a psychedelic pattern, is by Thomas, Germany. Condition is extremely important for value, especially with recent mass-produced pieces. Printed surface decoration can wear off, particularly if the item has been heavily used, so check that the design is crisp and clean. Also remember to count all the relevant elements. This set is missing one of its tumblers.

£35–45

glass

Although British street fashion and music were the ultimate in 1960s cool, Italian and Scandinavian designers led the way when it came to stylish glass. Italian glassmakers worked with a range of dense brilliant colours and smooth, untextured, typically thick-walled shapes to produce chic, sophisticated often witty glass that sat happily in their style-conscious interiors. Scandinavian designers clung to their "good taste/high quality" ethos in the face of the demand for fun design but were instrumental in the move towards the newly fashionable textured glass and cylindrical shapes that complemented the trend for hessian wallpaper and stacking domestic wares. Whitefriars was one of the few British glass companies to catch the style and mood with a range of coloured and textured glass. However, while many British manufacturers lay fallow, there was a growing number of talented young studio glass artists who arrived on the London scene in The Glasshouse at the very end of the decade.

◄◄ The reputation enjoyed by the Venini Glassworks (est. 1921) continued after the death in 1959 of its founder Paolo Venini, who had used early Venetian glassmaking techniques to create a stylish range of contemporary glass. Venini glass is keenly collected, and fakes are known. This large, handblown bowl was created for the firm c.1960 by Ludovico de Santillana and carries the mark "Venini, Murano, Italia".

£900–1000

◄◄ The popularity of Italian glass in the 1960s spawned a host of pieces by lesser-known and less prestigious workshops. Many Italian glassmakers left Italy after the war and moved to such farflung locations as Argentina (and even Blackpool!). The decanter (22¼in (57cm) tall) and vase shown have typically Italian exuberant colour and make playful reference to the traditional highly skilled Venetian techniques for producing striped effects in glass.

Left £75–85   Right £40–50

➠ Marks on glass are notoriously difficult to read – an eye-glass and the correct angle are essential – but they can transform the value of a piece. Both of these vases were made using the *sommerso* technique, developed by Venini c.1934, in which a thick outer layer of glass – either clear or coloured – covers an inner layer of ornamented or differently coloured glass. However, while the square-topped vase can only be identified as Murano glass, the blue vase carries the mark of a well-known Murano glassworks – the Seguso Vetri d'Arte.

Left **£45–65**   *Right* **£150–200**

➠ In the 1960s the cigarette had yet to be demonized and was still part of daily life. Almost every home boasted an ashtray, and heavy, stable glass ashtrays were both practical and aesthetically appealing. These ashtrays, made in Murano using the *sommerso* technique, had the extra cachet of bold colour and stylish design that was synonymous with Italian glass. They reflect the Italian predilection for the rounded organic smooth-walled shapes that formed one strand of the 1960s glass style.

£35–55 *Each*

➠ The variety of Italian glass encompassed quirky but high-quality pieces such as this cheeky blown-glass bird, designed by Alessandro Pianon (b.1931) and made in 1962 by Vistosi, one of the leading Venetian glassworks. Standing some 12in (32cm) high, it is one of a series of five rare and engaging metal-legged stylized chicks, all of which are eagerly collected as superb examples of the witty and engaging 1960s Italian design.

£800–1000

» The glass style of the 1950s had been dictated predominantly by inspired Scandinavian designers working for such firms as Orrefors (est. 1898) in Sweden. Ingeborg Lundin (b.1921) – the first woman designer at Orrefors – contributed to the firm's success in the 1960s. This bowl, which shows her use of blue and beige repeating geometric techniques, is part of the "Ariel" series, all of which are marked "Orrefors" and numbered. This bowl , made in 1966, is marked "Ariel 688a".

£900–1000

« The Holmegaard Glassworks dominated the Danish glass scene in the years after World War II. Their success was due largely to the designer Per Lutken, whose one-off experimental pieces are now classics and correspondingly priced. Far more accessible in terms of price and availability are these "Gulvases", designed by Otto Brauer, which were produced in various sizes and colours. Value will depend on size, and whether the bottle vases are cased (with white lining), or clear glass.

Cased green bottle £75–85   Clear blue bottle £35–45
Cased red bottle £100–120

» In the 1960s the Finnish glass designers who swept the board at the prestigious Milan Triennale in 1951 were preoccupied with the increasing democratization of design – they wanted to design glassware that was both useful, affordable and aesthetically pleasing. How far they succeeded can be seen in the undulating Lassi glass vases shown here, which were mass-produced in different colours by the Riihimaki glassworks (est. 1910).

£45–55 Each

➤ Ittala (est.1888) was one of the three major glassmaking companies that brought Finland to the front of glass design in the years following World War II. The firm owed its success to designers, such as Timo Sarpaneva (b.1926), who were able to create both highly sculptural exclusive and expensive pieces and a range of mass-produced, well-designed functional ware including the now highly collectable "i-glass" utility range manufactured in the 1960s. Any marked piece, such as the vase far right, will be particularly sought after among collectors. The small vase is by an unknown maker.

Vase (left) **£35–45**

Vase (right) **£65–85**

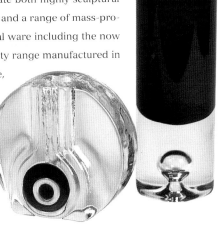

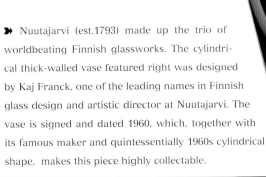

➤ Nuutajarvi (est.1793) made up the trio of worldbeating Finnish glassworks. The cylindrical thick-walled vase featured right was designed by Kaj Franck, one of the leading names in Finnish glass design and artistic director at Nuutajarvi. The vase is signed and dated 1960, which, together with its famous maker and quintessentially 1960s cylindrical shape, makes this piece highly collectable.

£300–350

◄ In Scandinavia, talented designers moved freely between the leading glassworks. Vicke Lindstrand (1904–83), who had been instrumental in developing the "Ariel" technique at Orrefors, also designed for the equally prestigious Kosta glassworks (est.1742). The thick-blown and cased vases seen here, made in 1962 and 1963, carry an etched mark "Kosta", together with the letters "LH", which show that they were made by Lindstrand. They also feature the serial numbers 1783 and 1763 – Lindstrand numbering begins at 1001.

Tall vase **£120–140**   *Round vase* **£160–180**

➤ One of the few English manufacturers to capture the spirit of the 1960s in glass was Whitefriars, thanks largely to Geoffrey Baxter, a young designer who joined fresh from the Royal College of Art in 1954. By the mid-1960s Baxter had introduced texture plus new colours and shapes, in a series of vases produced from moulds textured with brick, wire and bark. These included the Kingfisher-blue "Drunken Bricklayer's" vase shown above left (made in two sizes from 1967 until 1977), a tangerine vase with textured concentric circles (made 1967 until 1971) and the cylindrical "bark" vase shown far right, which was produced from 1967 until 1980 in three sizes, in a mould lined with rough oak bark.

Drunken Bricklayer's **£75–85** *Tangerine* **£55–65** *Textured* **£45–55** *Bark* **£25–35**

◀ In the 1950s, the British glassmaker Michael Harris left the Isle of Wight Glass Company and moved to Malta, where he set up Mdina Glass. And it was in Malta that he designed the purple vase shown here, which was initially produced c.1955 and continued in production until the late 1970s. Although it may have been produced in other colours, nearly all known examples are purple – one of the dominant colours in the 1960s psychedelic palette. Vases have survived in quantity, probably because they were less exposed to the daily rough and tumble than everyday domestic wares. If possible, check the insides for limescale deposits, which will feel rough to the touch and will detract from the appeal of the item.

£150–175

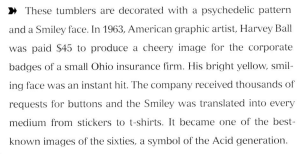

◄ Although the name Wedgwood is virtually synonymous with ceramics, the company also manufactured a range of glass – ornaments and paperweights in particular – and these blown "Bubble" vases with their heavy rounded bases look as though they could easily have doubled up on function. Made in 1965, they make no concession to colour or texture but nevertheless have a slightly quirky edge that is pure 1960s. Value is determined by size, shape and condition – flaws and damage are all too visible on clear glass.

Small **£40–50**   *Medium* **£50–60**
Large **£60–70**

▶ These tumblers are decorated with a psychedelic pattern and a Smiley face. In 1963, American graphic artist, Harvey Ball was paid $45 to produce a cheery image for the corporate badges of a small Ohio insurance firm. His bright yellow, smiling face was an instant hit. The company received thousands of requests for buttons and the Smiley was translated into every medium from stickers to t-shirts. It became one of the best-known images of the sixties, a symbol of the Acid generation.

£3–5 *Each*

◄ The Italian designer Joe Colombo's short life (1930–71) was dedicated to innovative design and pleasure, both of which come together in his range of "Assimetrico" glasses, which were expressly designed to allow you to hold a glass and a cigarette in one hand – the rounded stem fitted into the hollow of the palm and the bowl sat on the back of the hand. Designed in 1965, they were a slightly larger and modified version of the self-explanatory "Smoke" glasses – one of the first drinking glasses to move away from the traditional shape.

£150–250

metalware

A vogue for perfect geometric forms, especially circles and cylinders, dominated the design of metalware in the early part of the decade. The pre-eminence in this area of the Danish designers – established in the 1920s by Georg Jensen – was upheld in the 1960s by such masters as Arne Jacobsen, who was heavily influenced by his training as an architect. British silversmiths such as Robert Welch and David Mellor were interested in industrial design combined with craftsmanship and, under the sway of the Scandinavians, did much to exploit the potential of stainless steel. At the less-expensive end of the market, the Union Jack flag grew increasingly hard to avoid. It was incorporated in the design of many consumer goods, from biscuit tins to underpants. This outburst of patriotism was given a boost in April 1966 when *Time* magazine devoted its cover story to the phenomenon of "swinging London". Trend-setting companies such as Dodo Designs were quick to take advantage of the patriotic euphoria.

♠ The lid of this sleek coffeepot lies flush with its rim, forming a perfect cylinder. The pot is part of an award-winning range of stainless-steel tableware, the "Cylinda-Line", developed by the Danish architect and designer Arne Jacobsen (1920–71) for A.S. Stelton between 1964 and 1967. Danish creative genius is again evident in the "Caravel" range of silver flatware designed c.1960 by the sculptor Henning Koppel (1918–81) and made by the firm of Georg Jensen (est.1904). Koppel strove to produce silver that was "useful, and a joy to behold".

Coffeepot **£100–150** *Flatware* **£3000–3500**

◄ A subtle blend of angularity, gently curving surfaces and unusual details gives this stainless-steel tea-service its distinctive quality. Known as "Alveston", the range was designed in 1963 by silversmith Robert Welch (b.1929), who had first become interested in stainless steel during a visit to Scandinavia in the mid-1950s. Welch was consultant designer to the West Midlands stainless-steel manufacturer J. & J. Wiggin, which marketed its household products as "Old Hall Tableware". He occasionally collaborated with the Sheffield cutlery designer David Mellor (b.1930).

£300–350 *The set*

◄ Providing "pop-style playthings for adults" was the avowed intention of Dodo Designs, one of the leading firms in the field of Pop graphics, whose method was to apply bold, brightly coloured patterns to a variety of household goods. Dodo was one of small group of design companies that together with the fashion boutiques gave form to the lifestyle phenomenon of "Carnaby Street". The design of many of Dodo's accessories incorporated the Union Jack flag. The tin of knickers (unopened) are not by Dodo Designs, just pure Carnaby Street.

Tray and bin (each) **£60–100**

Knickers **£30–40**

♣ Style statements could even be made in the office. High-flying workers would plan their next moves while playing with "executive toys", such as this chrome "Newton's cradle", measuring 7¼in (18.5cm) high. The ball at either end could be lifted and released to hit the other balls, causing them all to rock in a mesmeric rhythm.

£15–20

textiles

"Today's in-crowd want homes as fashionable as the smart clothes they wear," declared *Ideal Home* magazine in 1966. Just like fashion, furnishing textiles swung and changed with the times. The early 1960s saw a taste for simple, abstract patterns; their geometric forms reflecting the straight, clean lines of contemporary architecture, the natural palette of oranges, browns and creams complementing a Scandinavian-look interior. With the Pop explosion in the mid-1960s, textiles reflected each passing fad. "This year's fabrics fall into two distinct groups," observed *Ideal Home* in 1966, "complex, geometrics influenced by the dizzy patterns of Op Art and flowing curvy florals, inspired by the Art Nouveau revival." As the decade progressed, designers drew on every source, from traditional Liberty prints to Andy Warhol paintings. Flower power and the hippy trail expressed itself in the growing demand for imported oriental rugs and also for home-produced oriental-style fabrics. Textile values depend on pattern, condition, size and designer. Selvages should have the name of manufacturer or artist and should be left intact when the fabric is made up.

◀◀ The development in the 1950s of mechanized screen-printing transformed the textile industry in the 1960s, enabling manufacturers to meet the demands of the new home owners who wanted stylish, modern designs. A notable firm was Heals, who marketed their fabrics through other shops and were an international force in modern textiles. The design on the left is called "Galleria" and the one on the right, "Ebbtide", both are by Barbara Brown (b.1932) for Heals.

£100–200

◀◀ Peter McCulloch was another designer working for Heals. This design is called "Signpost". The fabric is screen printed in the flat, bold colours that were at the forefront of printing technology in the early 1960s. These textiles became an emblem of a more flexible way of living and a rejection of the suburban values of the 1950s. Trips to Heals were a must for design-conscious newly-weds.

£100–200

« The striking graphics of this black-and-white design, "Geometri I", by the Danish designer Verner Panton (1926–98) are in the Op Art style so predominant from the mid-1960s. Op Art worked on the basis of fragmenting and distorting what the eye could see in an attempt to push visual perception to its limits. In this fabric, Panton's bold geometry is a far cry from the genteel restraint of floral prints of earlier in the century.

£200–400

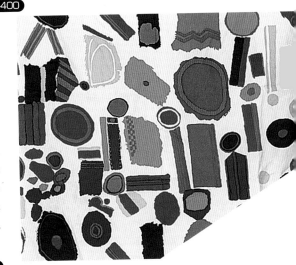

» This fabric, designed by Zandra Rhodes, features a repeat pattern of medals and military ribbons. Although these medals may have more in common with The Beatles' Sergeant Pepper (see p.119) than Sandhurst Military Academy, the military was a common theme in the 1960s, as it highlighted the general anxiety over the arms race. Rhodes is now best known for her couture lines and her pink hair.

£100–200

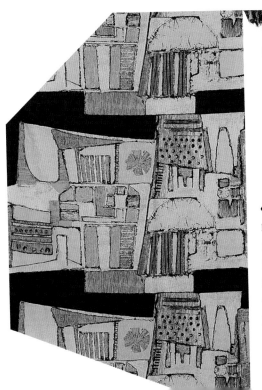

« ♣ After World War II the firm of David Whitehead (est. 1920s) became a pioneer in using artists to design textile patterns. In the 1960s the firm developed an internal design studio, thereby reacting quickly to fashion trends. The "Technicus" fabric by Merrick Hansel, left, was displayed at the 1969 Living Art exhibition. The "Age of Kings" fabric, was a commemorative design by Tibor Reich in 1964 for the RSC in Stratford and made by Tibor Ltd.

"Technicus" **£150–250**   "Age of Kings" **£300–400**

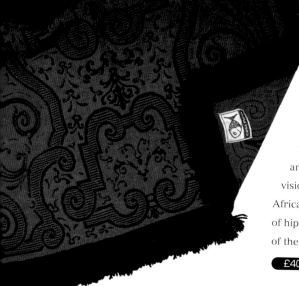

◀ Casa Pupo were retailers who imported exciting, original artefacts from the Mediterranean and the East. The rug shown left was a small-scale, inexpensive alternative to an antique Persian rug and absolutely perfect for the suburban opium den. The eclectic and personal style of Casa Pupo was the product of a specific 1960s vision of the world. It was the idea of a hippy trail leading to North Africa, the Far East and back to your home. The resulting style was a type of hippy baroque that was a symbolic rejection of the Modernist integrity of the 1950s.

£40–80

▶ The polished or painted floors of modern pads demanded small rugs to cover them. Scandinavia, particularly Finland, was known for its "Ryas", shaggy-pile rugs, hand-knotted from wool, rich in colour and often abstract in design. Cheaper machine-made copies were also available or do-it-yourself kits for the crafty housewife. Other options included sheep and goat skins and oriental rugs imported by the new hippy travellers.

£200–250

◀ The newly-introduced printing inks of the 1960s combined with roller printing and mechanized printing processes to create a wide range of innovative patterns and styles. The curtain fabric shown left with its orange colour and strong repeat graphic is highly characteristic of the period from 1968 until 1970. It is by an unknown designer. This bold pattern was probably intended for a large spread of drapes across a room or window.

£40–50

❱❱ These cushions reflect Pop Art, pop music and a global Pop culture. Andy Warhol immortalized the "Campbell's soup can" and this Heinz cushion reflects this Pop influence. The Beatles were the first band to capitalize on their fame with mass merchandise targeted at teeny-bopper fans across the world. The "Peace" symbol was designed for CND by Gerald Holtom in 1958 using the semaphore letters for N (nuclear) and D (defence). Adopted by students everywhere, it became one of the best-known symbols of the sixties.

Peace **£100–150**   *Beatles* **£15–25**   *Heinz* **£50–80**

❰❰ The jacket on the left is not valuable in itself but is a rare example of a textile designed by British designer Sue Thatcher. The design is called "Space walk" and was made c.1969 for Warner Fabrics Ltd to commemorate the moon landing. As a length of textile it would be more valuable, at around £500-800. The "British breakfast" shirt (right) dates from the same period. It typifies the humour of English Pop Art and was probably made for the King's Road boutique, "Mr Freedom".

"Space walk" **£300–500**   *"British breakfast"* **£200–250**

pictures and posters

In 1957 British painter Richard Hamilton famously defined Pop Art as: "popular, transient, expendable, low cost, mass-produced, young, witty, sexy, glamorous, big business..." thereby providing a manifesto for the new movement and also for the sixties Pop revolution. A young generation of artists from David Hockney to Andy Warhol, created fun and innovative pictures inspired by popular culture and quickly became as famous as pop stars themselves. Equally celebrated was a new breed of photographers such as David Bailey and Terence Donovan. Their dynamic images captured the mood of the time and celebrated the emerging popocracy of rock stars and models. However, the ultimate Pop Art form was the poster: typical student bedsit decoration and chosen medium of the Underground movement. Posters reflect sixties youth culture in all its transient glory.

♣ David Bailey was court photographer to the London scene of the 1960s. His photographs of fashion models and celebrities helped define swinging London as racy, glamorous and slightly dangerous. His "box of pin-ups" shown above, which contains 36 loose sheets featuring stylish black-and-white portraits, was published in 1965. The box is an archetypal example of the 1960s ideal of metropolitan celebrity.

£1200–2500

❝ Like weaving macramé hangings or making giant paper flowers, string pictures were a 1960s homecraft fad. A poor man's version of Op Art, they could be purchased either ready made or, for the nimble-fingered, in do-it-yourself kits. "It was a sort of trendy version of painting by numbers," remembers one enthusiast, "and just about as artistic." Although they might not be the ultimate in aesthetic creations, string pictures have their own kitsch value.

£20–30

◄◄ Signed Rosslyn and dated 1966, this picture is created with textured plaster on hardboard and finished with enamel paint. It typifies the period both in its rejection of traditional values of painting and drawing and its desire to unite art with craft. Inspired by artist Paul Klee, the three-dimensional, geometric shapes also reflect the influence of contemporary ceramics such as those produced by the Troika factory in Cornwall. Earthy colours, abstract patterns and a handmade look appeared in every form from paintings to textiles to pottery.

£90–120

★ Peter Blake (b.1932) is probably the most famous of the Pop artists who brought the cut-and-paste eclecticism of pin-ups, packaging and comics into fine art. Blake's best-known creation is the sleeve design for The Beatles album *Sergeant Pepper's Lonely Hearts Club Band*. This printed metal portrait of Babe Rainbow, a notorious lady wrestler, was created in 1968 for Dodo Designs, London.

£400–600

➤ Posters were the staple decoration of the student bedsit, encompassing every aspect of youth culture from political protest to the hedonistic pleasures of sex, drugs and rock and roll. "London – Come Wearing Just a Smile", with its blow-up nude, was designed by British illustrator Alan Aldridge (b.1943). The marijuana poster is American and created by Pandora Productions in 1969.

Posters (each) £200–400

73

♠ The print above is one of a set of four Beatles prints by Richard Avedon that was published under licence by the *Daily Express* as a set in 1967. The bright, acid oranges and yellows – the defining colours of the psychedelic movement at the end of the 1960s – could be achieved due to improved printing inks. Avedon – one of the world's most famous fashion photographers – was instrumental in establishing the fascination with celebrity figures that dominates the media today. The Jimi Hendrix poster above right is a famous design image from the end of the 1960s. Posters featuring such icons as Hendrix were popular in teenage bedrooms – few survived the hazardous conditions, and perfect examples are rare.

Beatles posters (set of four) **£700–900** *Hendrix poster* **£300–500**

➤ *Mister Tambourine Man* shown right is a poster homage to Bob Dylan by Martin Sharp, art director of the reactionary magazine *Oz*. This design first appeared as a cover of the magazine. Printed on foil paper, the poster was one of a series published by Sharp and his *Oz* colleagues in a venture called "Big O". The foil printing was a graphic appropriation of packaging technologies and caused a sensation in 1967.

£400–600

❰ In graphics, the language of psychedelia is based on a colour palette of hot yellows and reds as shown here. Posters such as these were the produce of a small group of artists and designers. This particular one was designed by Nigel Waymouth and Michael English a.k.a "Hapshash and the Coloured Coat", and produced for their shop "Granny Takes a Trip" in the King's Road.

£350–650

➤ This extremely large paper and cardboard wall mirror is a rare survivor of the disposable Pop furnishings that adorned the hippy pads. After the release of *Easy Rider*, mirror shades and tie-dyed shirts became the emblematic accessories to a hedonistic lifestyle that was nominally against consumerism and capitalism but nevertheless was wholly engaged with both.

£400–600

❰ The poster, far right, was designed by David Roe for an Isle of Wight pop concert. Roe was part of the "Poly Pops" design team at Paperchase. The poster is one of a series of four wrapping paper designs c.1969 that used pinball machines and juke boxes as their imagery. The Rolling Stones' tour poster of 1969 is by American graphic designer W. David Beyrd and based on an Art Nouveau original by Alphonse Mucha. The organic forms and unabashed eroticism of Art Nouveau were ideally suited to the hedonistic style of the psychedelic movement. This poster was probably sold at concert venues as part of the explosion of merchandising that was part of the rock scene in the late 1960s.

Lime-green poster **£50–60**

Stones poster **£250–350**

75

In the 1960s one of the best
ways that young people could express affiliation with the
new-found independence, the ground-breaking sexual liberation and
the burning desire to be different was through fashion. Inspired
by such arresting new faces as Twiggy (left) and Jean
Shrimpton, girls aspired to leanness, youthfulness and
pallor. While a father's self-esteem might have been
reflected in neatly clipped hair, respect for authority and
military bearing, his son – if he was a spirited boy –
would mimic The Beatles with their long floppy hair

fashion

and idiosyncratic clothes. "Is it a boy or is it a girl?" newspaper caption-writers were fond of asking. Influenced by
trendsetting designers, from London, to Paris and San
Francisco, and by mind-expanding drugs, which arguably
pushed their users' sense of daring to the limits, a multitude of
funky fashions came onto the scene. From the shortest space-
age mini-skirts to paisley frills, from kinky boots to spiky
"Winkle-pickers", and with even underwear and accessories being
transformed, there was a style to suit every streetwise young thing.

british design

"In New York it's the 'London Look', in Paris it's "*le style anglais*," boasted *Vogue* in 1965, as a young generation of British models, photographers and designers set the 1960s swinging. Jean "the Shrimp" Shrimpton and the boyish Twiggy became icons of female beauty. "Suddenly every girl with a hope of getting away with it is aiming to look not only under voting age but under the age of consent," said Mary Quant, pioneer of mini-skirts, high boots, trouser suits and a host of young styles that were all part of what she dubbed simply "the look". The new moving force in fashion was not Parisian haute couture but small London boutiques – Ossie Clark's Quorum, Lee Bender's Bustop, Barbara Hulanicki's Biba – started by young designers, blaring out rock music and selling "Pop" and "Op" clothes to mod boys and dolly birds. Carnaby Street became as busy a tourist site as Buckingham Palace, and at its peak Biba attracted 100,000 visitors a week. Inspired by teenage street style, the "Swinging London" look crossed continents and crashed through age barriers. "In the fifties girls dressed like their mothers," remembers one Chelsea girl. "In the sixties I wanted to look like Marianne Faithfull, and mummy wanted to look like me."

➤ Mary Quant (b.1934) opened her Bazaar boutique in King's Road, Chelsea, in 1955. She knew so little about business that she bought material retail at Harrods, but the garments she sewed in her bedsit were an instant hit. "I just happened to start when that 'something in the air' was coming to the boil," wrote Quant. "The clothes I made happened to fit exactly with the teenage trend, with pop records, espresso bars and jazz clubs." This Bazaar dress, with its dropped waist and short skirt, reflects the sharp and simple modern styles that character-ized the "Chelsea" look and made Quant the most famous clothes designer of her generation.

£100–150

❦ Forget Oxfam and feed Twiggy," read a 1960s car-bumper sticker. Lesley Hornby, at 5 feet 6 inches (167cm) tall and weighing only 91lbs (40kg), was the model who embodied the teenage revolution. "This is the Face of '66," trumpeted the *Daily Express*. "Twiggy – the Cockney Kid with the face to launch a thousand shapes, and she's only 16." Her waif-like look, short haircut and even her London accent were copied around the world, and she launched her own fashion line, designed by Pam Proctor and Paul Babb. This candy-striped dress is from the "Twiggy" range. Clothes were highly priced, at between 6 and 12 guineas, but an added incentive was the portrait hanger, free with each purchase and today collectable in its own right.

Dress £80–100

Hanger £35–40

◀◀ "Biba was a fantasy," said Barbara Hulanicki. Named after her sister, the first Biba boutique opened in Kensington in 1964, and soon teenagers were crowding into London's first communal changing room. Prices were low: a cotton mini-dress, such as the example shown on the left, sold for around £3. Hulanicki used vintage fabrics for both style and economy. The Biba shirt is made from a 1930s crepe, cut in a typically slim line. "In the sixties girls were prepared to suffer to look good: our long skinny sleeves were so tight they hindered circulation."

Dress **£50–70**   *Shirt* **£100–120**

▶▶ "I want to dress frilly people... in colours that confuse the eye," 23-year-old Ossie Clark told *Vogue* in 1965. Born in 1942 in Oswaldtwistle, Lancashire, Raymond ("Ossie") Clark rose from his northern working-class roots, through the Royal College of Art, to become "King of the King's Road" in the 1960s and 1970s. Clients of his Quorum boutique included stars such as Goldie Hawn and Mick Jagger, who gyrated in "Ossie" jumpsuits. The crepe dress on the right, made from a print designed by Clark's wife, Celia Birtwell, is a typically sensuous creation.

£200–250

"I want to dress frilly people"

◀◀ "The audience at the London premier of the hippy musical *Hair* seemed to be completely dressed by Thea Porter," noted a critic in 1969. Raised in Damascus, Porter (b.1927) was at the forefront of the ethnic fashion movement. Her Soho shop sold Eastern textiles, and her own designs were inspired by antique kaftans. Everyone from Princess Margaret to Elizabeth Taylor wore Porter dresses, attracted not only by their exoticism but also by their comfort, and the relief of being able to conceal rather than reveal every inch of flesh.

£125–175

french design

"Couture is for grannies," declared the actress Brigitte Bardot, and as a "youthquake" shook the world Paris adopted the "London" look. French mods were known as "*Yé-yés*" (from The Beatles' refrain "Yeah Yeah") and for the first time high fashion was influenced by street style. André Courrèges and Pierre Cardin launched the white-and-silver space-age look. Yves St Laurent made mini-dresses based on Mondrian paintings. Paco Rabanne clothed his models in plastic and metal chainmail. For some it was all too much – Balenciaga, Paris's most classical designer, retired in 1968, the year of student revolution, claiming that haute couture was dead. Designers had to adapt to survive, introducing more affordable, ready-to-wear lines while still publicizing their names with increasingly avant-garde catwalk shows. "Is Courrèges wearable?" demanded *Life* magazine in 1965. At the time, it was a revolutionary question to ask about Parisian fashions, but from the 1960s onwards the concept of fantastic, provocative unwearability became central to the very notion of haute couture.

◄◄ Chief designer at Dior from 1962, Mark Bohan created new young lines such as "Dior Sport" and introduced a simpler, much more modern construction. "Day looks are concise, functional, basically pyramid shaped," said *Vogue* in 1966. This A-line apple-green dress by Dior reflects the fashionable geometric style, its "mini-jupe" divided into culottes. Shorts, knickerbockers, culottes and pantsuits all hit the catwalks in the 1960s, but long after the tiniest skirts became acceptable women in trousers were refused entry to smart restaurants.

£300–400

◄◄ Not every couturier jumped on the teenage bandwagon. "When in doubt, wear a Chanel," advised *Vogue*. Jackie Kennedy, First Lady of the USA and fashion icon, wore designs by Coco Chanel (1883–1971) as well as those by Hubert de Givenchy (b.1927). This yellow brocaded cocktail dress, designed by Givenchy, reflects the more formal styles of the early 1960s and the straight-lined simplicity of the designer whose creative muse was the actress Audrey Hepburn, the epitome of style and elegance.

£250–300

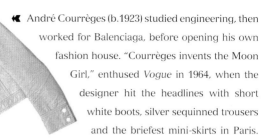

◄◄ André Courrèges (b.1923) studied engineering, then worked for Balenciaga, before opening his own fashion house. "Courrèges invents the Moon Girl," enthused *Vogue* in 1964, when the designer hit the headlines with short white boots, silver sequinned trousers and the briefest mini-skirts in Paris. This padded dress reflects his move away from the traditional waisted silhouette. It is fastened with poppers, which, like zips, became a popular feature. The plastic biker-style jacket, labelled "Couture Future", shows how Courrèges adapted male fashions and man-made materials to create a brand new women's wardrobe.

Dress **£550–650** *Jacket* **£250–300**

➤➤ "You are going to see some slightly strange girls and boys," Pierre Cardin told visitors to the showing of his 1966 collection. Known as the "*Fauve*" ("Wild One"), Cardin (b.1922) pioneered space-age style, clothing his models in cat-suits, cut-out dresses and astronaut-like helmets. He promoted his sci-fi fantasies with commercial acumen. Cardin was among the first Paris designers to sell ready-to-wear in chain stores. The coat-dress on the right was designed for Miss Selfridge, the new young branch of the London department store, Selfridges, with which Cardin signed a contract in 1966.

£40–60

◄◄ "The only new frontier left in fashion is finding new materials," claimed the Spanish-born designer Paco Rabanne (b.1934), who trained as an architect before becoming one of Paris's most futuristic couturiers. By 1966 Rabanne was using an estimated 30,000 metres of Rhodoid plastic a month in his creations. The tunic with matching mini-skirt is made from leather and metal. Rabanne's chain belt became a favourite accessory. His signature chainmail dresses were harder to wear, needing a body stocking for decency and comfort. Described as "wearable sculptures", they tend to be collected as design classics rather than as clothing.

Dress **£400–600** *Belt* **£100–150**

fun fashion

The young were the trendsetters of the 1960s, and by the middle of the decade half the clothes in Britain were being sold to people aged between 14 and 19. "Once only the rich, the Establishment, set the fashion," claimed Mary Quant in 1965. "Now it is the inexpensive little dress seen on the girls in the high street." Suburban mod styles were adopted by the Chelsea set, and swinging London's teenagers, both inspired and plundered the wardrobes of the world, trying everything from Parisian space-age fashions and Afghan coats to vintage clothes purchased for pennies from Portobello market. "Looks changed with the batting of a false eyelash," recalls one 1960s model. "We'd wear anything – and sometimes almost nothing!" The boutiques in Carnaby Street and King's Road became stylistic and social melting pots. "Snobbery has gone out of fashion," added Quant, "and in our shops you will find duchesses jostling with typists to wear the same dress." The most famous little 1960s dress was the mini. "Brevity is the soul of fashion," reported *Vogue*.

⬆ Abstract painting, Op Art and Pop Art filtered through to fashion. Yves St Laurent's Mondrian-inspired dresses and black-and-white geometric shifts inspired countless imitators, and the green-and-white dress in nylon jersey, above right, is a high-street version of the latest Parisian style. The striped dress, above left, is labelled "Liza Peta, Made in England". No pop-music programme was complete without its energetically twisting and jiving go-go dancers, typically attired in space-age mini-dresses such as these, hipster belts and white plastic boots.

£35–40 *Each*

◀ Dresses were reduced not just in terms of length. Designers experimented with transparent fabrics and cut-outs. One of the hottest looks of the mid-1960s was the bikini dress with a see-through midriff, pioneered by British designer John Bates. On this American version by Dune, the top is attached to the skirt by metal clips. The logical extension of these increasingly invisible pieces was the topless dress, launched by the Californian designer Rudi Gernriech, which in 1964 led to three London girls being arrested for indecency.

£55–65

➤ Like the blow-up chair, the paper dress reflected a throw-away consumer culture. The floral example on the right is by the American stationery company Hallmark. "Shorten with scissors to the desired length," say the instructions. The manufacturers claimed the item was flame-resistant, and paper dresses never caught fire in the market-place either, proving, like paper underpants, only a short-lived novelty. This, combined with their built-in obsolescence and iconic 1960s appeal, makes surviving examples rare and collectable today.

£150–220

◄ "What is the erogenous zone of our present fashion period?" the *Guardian* asked Mary Quant in 1967. "The crotch," she responded. "Clothes are designed to lead the eye to it." The mini-suit by Smart Miss, left, is so short that it barely covers the bottom. "It will enable girls to run faster, and because of it they may have to," said Mayor John Lindsay, when the style hit New York. Soon, even older women were shortening their skirts, and the mini was on sale everywhere. The pale blue and white floral dress bears the Marks & Spencer house label, St Michael.

Dress £20–25   *Suit* £30–40

"We'd wear anything – and sometimes almost nothing!"

➤ Crochet dresses came into fashion in the mid-1960s. "Every girl had a little crochet number," remembers a 1960s teenager. "It was the ultimate dolly-bird dress. The only problem was what to wear underneath it. Unless you really wanted to let everything hang out, you had to get one of those new, flesh-coloured body stockings." The classic version was a white, figure-hugging mini-dress, its reduced length and generous supply of holes leaving little to the imagination. The longer shift dress on the right dates from later in the decade, reflecting the more relaxed hippy style. The crochet shoulder bag was a popular ethnic accessory – this example is decorated with fringing and wooden beads and still smells faintly of patchouli.

Bag £10–20   *Dress* £20–25

◄◄ Born in Naples in 1914, Marchese Emilio Pucci di Barsento was a bomber pilot and Olympic skier before he turned his attention to sportswear after World War II. He reached his height of popularity in the 1960s when clients such as Mick Jagger and Jackie Kennedy flocked to buy his boldly patterned silk clothing. In the seventies however, his extravagent style fell from fashion and many simply threw away their psychedelic shirts making surviving examples very collectable. Pucci designs were much imitated, so check for the Pucci label and a signature on the patterned silk.

£200–250

"It all adds up to the Total Look"

➤ Mary Quant pioneered the use of PVC in fashion although, as she reflected in her autobiography, it did not always pay to be first. Initial experiments proved disastrous; the poly vinyl chloride melted over her machinery and perforated seams ripped like postage stamps. It took nearly two years for techniques to be perfected. Quant persevered and like the "Tonik" suit and the mini-skirt, the plastic mac became one of the fashion icons of the sixties. This example, in fashionable Mary Quant-style black and white, is labelled "Mist-O-Skye – made in Scotland."

£30–40

◄◄ Labelled "Gina Tereso, made in British Hong Kong", this acrylic, vinyl-trimmed top provides a mass-produced version of Cardin's 1966 cosmonaut look. Models were dressed in short jersey tabards decorated with a patent target, and worn with boots and skull caps with pastic visors. "Rather a shock", commented the Observer newspaper on viewing these proto-Star Trek fashions. "You see I was right," boasted Cardin when he watched the moon landing in 1969 and teenagers embraced this mod look.

£25–30

◀◀ Bell bottoms were inspired by sailors' trousers. Early versions, made from itchy navy serge, had a flap at the front which buttoned up on each side. You could buy them for almost nothing in army surplus stores and imagine that you were simultaneously mocking imperialism and making a fashion statement. As an alternative, jeans and trousers with ordinary legs were butchered up to the knee at side seams so that triangles of new cloth could be inserted to create flares. The arrival of platform soles made it necessary to sew another deep band all around the bottom of the new flares to avoid the 'half-mast' look. Commercial makers soon caught on, and "loons" were all the rage for a few years. Meanwhile, in the sunny, surfing, beach culture of California, the shortest shorts were the height of fashion.

Flares £25–35 *Shorts* £25–30

"Fashion... should be mass-produced"

▶▶ "Rightly or wrongly, I have been credited with the Lolita Look, the Schoolgirl Look, the Wet Weather Look, the Kinky Look, the Good Girl Look," wrote Quant in 1966. "I want to be first with a lot more." Perhaps the most famous designer of the period, Quant's clothes are very collectable today. In addition to the Bazaar Boutique, she and her husband, Alexander Plunket-Greene, launched the Ginger Group in 1963 to create a mass-produced version of "the Look". This red and purple jersey dress has a Ginger Group label. While big names such as Quant and Biba are becoming increasingly collectable, non-designer clothing such as this purple lace mini-dress (manufacturer unknown), can still be picked up very cheaply from fleamarkets.

Dress £200–300 *Mini* £15–20

85

➤ This chiffon cocktail dress, by Marie Laure, Paris, reflects the more formal evening fashions of the early sixties. The tight-fitting, knee-length shift was perfect for the Twist – the dance craze that took off along with the new discotheques. "The Twist is above all a dance for the very young," warned George Melly, "danced badly by the middle-aged it becomes obscene..." The trailing panels at the back were designed to set off a twisting rear and this dress would have been worn with stilettos and backcombed hair.

£25–30

◀ Space-age style inspired a fashion for shiny, metallic fabrics particularly in evening wear. This sequinned top, labelled "Made within the British Empire", provided an affordable high street approximation of Paris fashions. The gold and silver brocade waistcoat is by Biba and also came in a man's version. On Biba's earliest works, labels were white, with simple modern black graphics. The black and gold embroidered label shown here, designed by John McConnell c.1968, typified the glamour of Barbara Hulanicki's designs. In the seventies, printed black and gold labels were used.

Waistcoat £100–180   Top £35–40

➤ The mini dress was blamed for everything from the moral decline of the nation's youth to an increase in traffic accidents, as male drivers' eyes were distracted from the road by female thighs. One change it certainly effected was in tax regulation. Previously skirts under 24 inches long were classed as children's clothing and exempt from purchase tax. Confronted by shrinking hemlines, such as this velvet evening dress which barely covers the bottom, regulations were changed, From 1st January 1966, women's clothes were assessed for taxation purposes, no longer by length but by bust size.

£15–20

❧ "Evening dressing is a matter of choice," declared Vogue in 1966, noting the fashion for everything from the briefest minis to full-length gowns. The silk jersey dress (right) is by Emilio Pucci. The cotton shift decorated with bright flowers (centre) is from Bernshaw of Mayfair. "Long dresses with big prints and a fashionable halter neck are worn with long flowing hair and dangly earrings," advised Vogue. The Liberty-style print dress with a high neck (maker unknown), reflects the new Romanticism that replaced the hard-edged mod look in the late sixties. Designers drew their influences from Art Deco, Art Nouveau and an idealized rural past, most famously epitomized by Laura Ashley (1925-85), who transformed the Chelsea girls into Victorian milkmaids – their short hairstyles and shorter Op Art mini-skirts, replaced by flowing hair and flower-sprigged maxis, that brought a trailing end to the swinging sixties.

Patterned dress **£20–25**　　*Floral dress* **£30–50**　　*Pucci dress* **£250–325**

"Reminiscent of a one-night stand: forgettable, disposable, and possibly slightly embarrassing the next day"

hippy style

"The Kooky Kids of '66 have been replaced by the Flower Girls of '67. Swinging London is awash with Hippie Fashion," reported the *Daily Mirror* in the summer of 1967. Whereas Britain set the look for the first half of the decade, hippy style emerged from the West Coast of the USA in the mid-1960s. San Francisco was the capital of flower power; a musical, sartorial and social movement that soon blossomed across the world. "Turn on, tune in and drop out," urged LSD guru, Dr Timothy Leary. Experimentation with psychedelic drugs found expression in multi-coloured, often home-made clothing such as tie-dyed shirts, patchwork velvet dresses and embroidered jeans. Rejecting western consumerism, young travellers took to the hippy trail, adopting Eastern religions and ethnic fashions. Joss-stick-scented boutiques sprang up on every high street and were filled with a cultural hotchpotch of Indian kaftans, vintage clothes and protest t-shirts — unisex styles worn by a new generation of long-haired, love-beaded, patchouli-smelling boys and girls who, as their shocked parents complained, were becoming increasingly indistinguishable.

◄◄ Hippy style was a boon for sweatshop owners with piles of remnants available to make patchwork designs. This pair of jeans has been been transformed into a skirt with inset panels of a variety of floral fabrics. Jumble sales and markets were a mine of inspiration. "We used to cut up old scarves, '30s dresses and chenille curtains and make them into patchwork clothes," remembers one former hippy. The Neo-medieval style of the drawstring top on the right, reflects fashions at the turn of the decade.

Skirt £40–45   *Top* £15–20

◄◄ The kaftan was worn by men as well as women. Some girls made their own garments for next to nothing, as such loose-fitting styles required little sharp tailoring. This one is by Marion Foale and Sally Tuffin, students from the Royal College of Art who began producing clothes in 1960. Foale and Tuffin pioneered pan suits, hipsters and Pop Art dresses. They were also amongst the first to rediscover prints from Liberty & Co. and, as here, transform them into clothes for the young.

£15–30

➤ Interest in Native American culture was expressed in the fringed buckskin, perhaps most memorably worn by Roger Daltry of The Who at the Woodstock festival in 1969, when he whipped his fringes into a veritable frenzy. The Afghan coat – embroidered suede lined with sheepskin or goat's hair – became a fashion cliché but inadequate curing led to its own problems: "My afghan was so smelly that my teacher wouldn't let it into the classroom," remembers one 1960s girl.

Tassel **£35–45**   *Sheepskin* **£30–40**

◄ Imports of gaudily decorated jackets, often woven with as many legends as a Turkish carpet, appealed to male peacocks and earth mothers alike. Cheesecloth shirts, harem pants and cheap, embroidered kaftan shirts such as this one, which sold for about £3, were available through mail order in the music papers. The Mexican-inspired poncho, was also a favourite. This example is embroidered with messages of peace and love and was made in Greece, a favourite European stop on the hippy trail.

Top **£15–20**   *Poncho* **£25–35**

➤ The "557XX" Levi jacket, known as the "Trucker Jacket" was designed in 1962 and introduced the now familiar pointed pocket flaps, emphasized by V-shaped seams. Side pockets were later added to this design. Vintage jeans are rare, and these original 1960's Levis are in good condition, hence their value. Collectors refer to such items as "Capital E's" from the red tab on the pocket inscribed "LEVIS". After 1971, a lower-case "e" was used. Both inexpensive and highly priced versions can be found, but desirability is determined by such detail as the stitching, brass rivets and pockets.

Jacket **£150–200**   *Jeans* **£300–350**

lingerie and swimwear

"Bras have been like something you wear on your head on New Year's Eve," commented fashion designer Rudi Gernreich in 1965. The decade that saw the launch of the topless dress and culminated with women burning their bras was not a golden age for controlling underwear. The boned girdles and conical brassieres of the 1950s gradually gave way to soft, unstructured lingerie that complemented rather than moulded the shape of the female body, contributing to a nude look. Gernreich pioneered the flat, unwired "no-bra" bra. Twiggy, who had a 30½in (77.5cm) bust, called her sheer nylon bra and brief set "Starkers". As skirts grew ever shorter, stockings and suspenders were supplanted by pantyhose. "In European countries where they ban mini-skirts in the streets and say they're an invitation to rape, they don't understand about stocking tights underneath," said Mary Quant, who began producing underwear in 1965. She commissioned her first fashion tights from a dance-wear manufacturer, and soon pantyhose were the latest mod craze, available in every style and pattern from lacy and floral to Lurex and Op Art. The fashion for matching legs with mini-skirts to create a "total look" even sparked a summertime cosmetics trend: *Vogue* advised applying rouge to the knees, and Coty produced leg make-up in pastel shades to imitate coloured tights. During the 1967 summer of love, carefree, back-to-nature hippies dispensed with clothing altogether, but some covered their nakedness with decorative body painting.

⬆ Underwear, like outerwear, was decorated with bold designs, as exemplified by this American bra and girdle. While more mature women clung to their foundations, the younger ones wanted new-look lingerie. "I simply hate suspenders; to me they look like some sort of fearful surgical device," said Mary Quant. As the mini-skirt came in, stockings were replaced by tights. Lycra, invented in 1958, stimulated the development of body stockings and light bra and panty sets, such as this Quant example, which were invisible under even the tightest clothes. The abandonment of controlling underwear became a symbol of female liberation, but the idealization of natural, youthful beauty brought new constraints with the growth of the diet craze.

Floral bra £16–18   *Set by Quant* £4–5
Girdle £20–25

➤ Invented in 1938, nylon – washable, cheap and often colourful – was a hugely popular material, particularly for nightwear and lingerie. "Nylon night-dresses had several transparent floaty layers," remembers one 1960s mother. "You'd wake up with one of the layers wrapped round your head all hot and sweaty." The "babydoll" nightie, often complete with matching underpants, took its name from the eponymous 1956 film starring Carroll Baker as a child bride. The nylon slip on the far right is decorated with a bright psychedelic pattern in the style of Pucci prints.

Nightie **£10–12** *Slip* **£10–12**

◀ These two suits illustrate changing styles in swimwear. Homemade from a 1960s Op Art fabric, the black-and-white cotton swimsuit on the far left, with its generous, skirted shape, still reflects 1950s fashions. As the 1960s progressed, swimwear became more revealing, as shown by the backless, sideless example in colourful clinging nylon (near left). Designer Rudi Gernreich took this look still further with his 1964 topless swimsuit. "Bikinis have reached the minimum... so they've become boring," said Mary Quant in 1967, claiming that the way forward was body tattoos and perhaps three triangles of stick-on fabric.

Skirted suit **£12–16** *Cut-out suit* **£15–25**

➤ Stockings and tights of the 1960s are collected as packaged items rather than as wearable clothing. This selection is unopened, and values reflect the faces depicted. "Inspired by Twiggy for the Now People," say the words on the package of the Twiggy nylons by Trimfit USA. The "Beatles" stockings in the centre, sought after today by Beatles' fans, were made in England by Ballito, and the stocking tops are printed with the faces and signatures of the Fab Four. On the Beatles mini pantyhose (far right), the contents and packaging are undecorated, so the price range is lower.

Nylons **£15–20** *Stockings* **£160–200** *Pantyhose* **£20–25**

hats, shoes and bags

"These boots are made for walkin'... " began the refrain of a hit song by Nancy Sinatra. Once an item of purely functional footwear, the boot became the ultimate 1960s fashion accessory, worn with a mini-skirt, carrying overtones of fetishism, and available in every style and colour. The fashion designer André Courrèges popularized white space-age ankle boots; Honor Blackman, in the cult television series *The Avengers*, wore long, sexy black-leather "kinky boots" (recording a single of the same name); and Mary Quant managed to make even gumboots trendy. Shoes changed dramatically, the pointed stilettoes of the early 1960s giving way to round-toed, little-girl "flatties", set off with textured or patterned tights, while the end of the decade saw the rise of the platform sole, which kept maxi-skirts and flared trousers from trailing on the ground. In the 1950s, no lady would have dreamed of being seen in town without hat and gloves. In the 1960s, the fashions for bouffant, back-combed hair, elaborate hairpieces and asymmetric hair-dos banished the hat from everyday wear. Handbags were also affected by the changing styles, and the long-strapped shoulder bag, which freed women's hands, became a symbol of the blissfully liberated, swinging 1960s.

❦ "Courrèges clothes are so beautiful," artist Andy Warhol told *Vogue*. "Everyone should look the same dressed in silver. Silver doesn't look like anything. It merges into everything." In 1964 Courrèges exhibited his "moon girl" collection. In a plain-white showroom, moving to the beat of tom-tom drums, tall athletic models wore the shortest of mini-skirts, silver-spangled trousers and white, ankle-length boots. White, silver and gold became the colours of the moment, and fashions by Courrèges were endlessly copied – so much so that the designer eventually refused to admit the press or retail fashion buyers to his couture shows. The accessories below are high-street versions of space-age style, including silver plastic boots with a red psychedelic lining made by Party of Sussex, a silver rainhat, and gold Lurex ankle boots labelled "Tender Tootsies, Canada".

Knee boots £30–40   *Rainhat* £8–10
Ankle boots £15–20

➤ With its rainy climate and love of outdoor pursuits, Britain already had a long tradition of high-quality waterproof wear. The "Wellington" boot took its name from the Duke of Wellington, but it was Mary Quant who transformed it into a fashion item. Quant experimented with PVC (polyvinyl chloride) and her "wet-weather" look brought plastic macs to the catwalk. The short, red gumboots with ring-pull zips were made from injection-moulded plastic. Quant's logo is moulded into the heel, so that a wearer walking on soft ground in the rain would leave left a little trail of daisy prints behind her.

£50–60

"These boots are made for walkin'..."

◄◄ American experiments with leather substitutes resulted in the development of "Corfam", simulating patent leather and sparking the "wet" look. Although the calf-clinging look was the height of fashion, boots such as the pair shown were hard to put on, requiring slippery nylon stockings and lots of talcum powder. In 1969 Biba made knee-length platform boots in plum-and-chocolate suede, which "zipped so tightly that they stopped the blood flow", according to Biba owner, Barbara Hulanicki. Customers were undeterred, and in the first three months Hulanicki sold 75,000 pairs.

£25–45

❦ Courrèges's little white boots became one of the fashion clichés of the 1960s. The white plastic pair are American, with a label reading: "Hi Brows – as worn by the girls on *Hullabaloo.*" *Hullabaloo* (1965–6) was an American pop TV programme broadcast by NBC, enlivened by a resident troupe of mini-skirted, ankle-booted "go-go" dancers. These shoes are old stock and unworn, which increases their value. As well as condition, size also affects the desirability of vintage footwear; since each new generation grows bigger and taller, fewer people can wear the smaller sizes of the past.

£75–85

93

➤ In the early 1960s, shoes still bore 1950s features such as "winkle-picker" toes and sharp stiletto heels, as shown in the red pair on the right. But in the USA Abigail Van Buren, author of the "Dear Abby" syndicated column, launched a campaign against shoe manufacturers, backed up by thousands of readers' letters. The protestors demanded that manufacturers should "liberate the captive feet of womanhood" from the agonies of needlepoint shoes. As the teenage look came in, shoes too became girlish, with "Mary Jane" straps and rounded or squared toes. Heels were either thick and solid or flat. "It is not logical... to walk all day on 3 inch heels," said André Courrèges. "Heels are as absurd as the bound feet of ancient Orientals."

£20–25 *Each*

❦ Imprisoned in tight-fitting boots and hot plastic shoes, 1960s feet were in sore need of liberation. British pop singer Sandy Shaw hit the headlines for performing in bare feet, and by the end of the decade the hippies and flower people had also cast off traditional footwear in favour of naked toes and open sandals. Roman sandals, such as the white pair with tapes going up the leg, complemented mini-skirts and were a popular style – but impractical, since the ties would come undone unless they were so tight as to restrict circulation. The sandals bottom left are labelled "Biarritz", and decorated with the ubiquitous, Mary Quant-style, black-and-white plastic flowers.

£20–30 *Each*

➤ "Clip us on your Scholl Sandals," read the words on the packaging of these colourful plastic flowers. William Scholl, a doctor and shoemaker's grandson, began selling footcare products in 1904. Dr Scholl "Exercise" sandals, with beechwood bases and leather straps, were launched in 1965 and sold at drugstores. "Undo the harm that fashion shoes do," advised the ads. To the company's surprise, the therapeutic sandals became fashionable and were later manufactured in a host of trendy colours with funky clip-ons.

£5–8

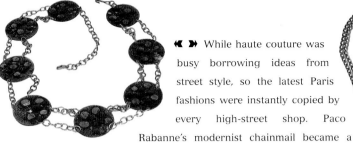

"Liberate the captive feet of womanhood"

◀ ▶ While haute couture was busy borrowing ideas from street style, so the latest Paris fashions were instantly copied by every high-street shop. Paco Rabanne's modernist chainmail became a favourite look, most easily worn in the form of light metallic shoulder bags, such as the silver mesh example on the right, and the ubiquitous chain-link belt shown above left. The belt, with enamel copper disks, was made by Renoir/Matisse, the Californian company known from the 1950s for their artistically enamelled, modern copper jewellery.

Belt **£50–60** *Bag* **£20–25**

❧ Pop Art and Op Art had an enormous influence on fashion, and by the middle of the decade it was possible to accessorize a black-and-white PVC coat with a two-tone plastic bag (left) and shoes. The flat-heeled "dolly" look, epitomized by the trendy mix-and-match plastic patent mules (right), was most famously modelled by Twiggy, with her long matchstick-thin legs and size 4½ feet (37½ in continental European sizes). "The papers all wanted me to be the... gawky little girly standing knock-kneed and pigeon-toed with my tongue hanging out," she recalled.

Bag **£55–65** *Shoes* **£25–30**

◀ Developments in plastics technology in the 1960s led to the production of affordable footwear in every shape and colour, as well as doing much to promote the use of foot-powders and deodorants. Shown with a matching red-plastic, gilt-handled handbag by Ackery, London, these bright-red patent shoes are typical of period design, with their squared-off toes, straight broad heels and large gilt buckle. As middle-aged women abandoned their stilettoes and adopted the more comfortable, childish shoe shapes first worn by their daughters, so the young looked for new and different designs. Arriving in the late 1960s and towering into the 1970s, the platform literally became the height of youthful fashion.

Bag **£10–15** *Shoes* **£18–22**

❦ Shoulder bags had been popular during World War II. They had been issued to the women's forces, and their practical design – which freed the hands and was suitable for carrying a gas mask – was echoed in civilian styles. The 1950s saw the return of the ladylike handbag, a complement to the wide-skirted, hourglass shape of "New Look" fashions. In the 1960s, as women adopted trousers and straight short dresses, shoulder bags came back into vogue. As with the mini-skirt, both Mary Quant and André Courrèges were credited with reintroducing them. The brown-leather bag with gilt chain-link strap and trim is by Paco Rabanne. The patterned silk bag with the gilt chain is by Italian couturier Emilio Pucci. As is the case with all fashion items and accessories, bags should be checked for a label or signature. Expect to pay more for bags by big-name designers such as these.

Pucci bag **£155–175**   *Rabanne bag* **£150–175**

"Go dotty this spring"

➤ "Totalization!" advised *Vogue* in 1965. "Tops, mini-skirts, tights and shoes all totally matching." Fashion designer Rudi Gernreich spearheaded the "total" look, encouraging women to dress from top to toe in matching patterns. Designers produced hosiery reflecting the decorations of their latest look, and shoes and bags followed suit. The raffia bag with leather spots is by Calderon. In 1965 *Vogue* noted the fashion for shoes decorated with large dots resembling ping-pong balls; the pair on the right with the distinctive round heels dates from the same period. Influenced by Op Art, spotty fashions became very popular in the mid-1960s. "Go dotty this spring," read the words of one advertisement. Even cosmetics manufacturers joined in, suggesting that women paint their faces with artificial freckles.

Bag **£30–40**   *Shoes* **£25–35**

➤ Though no longer *de rigeur*, hats were still worn by society ladies and for smart events. Jackie Kennedy popularized the "pill box", and the early 1960s saw a fashion for hats made from artificial flowers, such as the yellow example (left): "like putting your head in a giant chrysanthemum," enthused *Vogue*. Wigs and teased hair led to high-domed styles, which could be slipped on over a bouffant hairdo. The flowerpot hat (above left) reflects the new geometric designs, while the brown model is typical of the helmet shape introduced by Courrèges. Soft caps, in various styles, from tweed ones inspired by François Truffaut's film *Jules et Jim* to John Lennon's fisherman's hat, were popular with teenagers. The green "scooter" hat has an integral scarf so it can be tied on while you are riding your Lambretta.

Yellow £20–30   *Flowerpot* £40–50   *Brown* £25–35   *Green* £8–12

◂ The word psychedelic comes from the Greek *psyche* ("mind") and *deloun* ("to reveal"). It was coined by the hippy generation to describe the mind-expanding experiences induced by hallucinogenic drugs. Psychedelic patterns were initially an anti-establishment style typified by Underground music posters and Ken Kesey's multicoloured bus, but they were adopted by the commercial design industry and were soon swirling over everything from food packaging to fashion accessories. The matching vinyl travel set epitomizes late-1960s psychedelic fever, when, stylistically at least, you could "tune in, turn on and drop out" in every high-street store. Such wildly patterned, colourful sets are particularly collectable.

The set £50–70

97

cosmetics

"Make-up – old style – is out", claimed Mary Quant. "It is used as expertly as ever but it is designed not to show. The ideal now is to have a baby skin untouched by cosmetics." As youthful fashions came in, sales of moisturiser boomed and a natural "no make-up" look was aided with new, thinner foundations and pan sticks. The fifties scarlet mouth was replaced by pale pink or white lips (manufacturers added titanium to give lipstick an irridescent gloss). The best-selling lipstick for teenage girls was Miner's The Palest. Lips contrasted with dark, exaggerated eyes, "there you can use the lot," said Quant, "eye shadow, eye liner and lashings of mascara plus false eyelashes – even false eyebrows I should think." Twiggy even painted freckles onto her face. Quant and Twiggy helped popularize the fashion for short geometric haircuts that could be embellished with wigs or hairpieces, but by the end of the decade real hair was back. The trailing locks and afro styles adopted by both sexes became a symbol of the hippy revolution, epitomized by the famous flower-power musical: *Hair*.

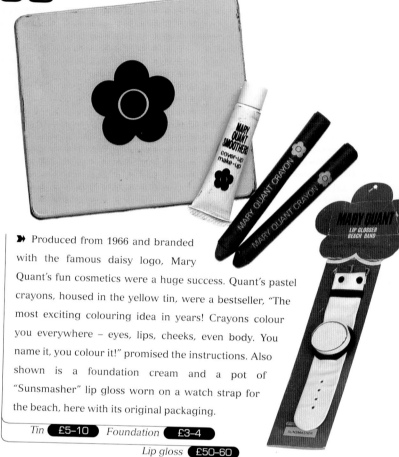

➤ Produced from 1966 and branded with the famous daisy logo, Mary Quant's fun cosmetics were a huge success. Quant's pastel crayons, housed in the yellow tin, were a bestseller, "The most exciting colouring idea in years! Crayons colour you everywhere – eyes, lips, cheeks, even body. You name it, you colour it!" promised the instructions. Also shown is a foundation cream and a pot of "Sunsmasher" lip gloss worn on a watch strap for the beach, here with its original packaging.

Tin **£5–10**   Foundation **£3–4**

Lip gloss **£50–60**

◀ Cathy McGowan, "Queen of the Mods" and presenter of television's, *Ready Steady Go*, was a fashion icon for teenagers. "The girls aped Cathy's long hair and eye-covering fringe," remembers Barbara Hulanicki, "and soon their little white faces were growing heavy with stage make-up, lids weighed down with doe-like thick lashes." "Cathy's Survival Kit" (a portable make-up set) is collectable today as a piece of pop ephemera.

£60–80

➤ False eyelashes were essential for the 1960s face: "They looked like enormous spiders," noted Jean Shrimpton. "We bought them in long strips and cut off a length and stuck the strips above our own lashes." Twiggy sported up to three sets at once. "But if you wore them on the upper and lower lashes, they had an unfortunate tendency to lock together," remembers one magazine editor, "and they were always falling off and sticking to your clothes." This selection includes "Mod Perma-Lash" by Andrea (individual stick-on lashes), "Big Fluttery Lashes" for children, a 1960s eyelash tint and "Hoodwinks", false lashes packaged in a box.

False eyelashes (each) **£3-6**
"Hoodwinks" **£20-30**

➤ During the mid-1960s there was a huge craze for false hair. Woolworth's sold synthetic hairpieces for as little as £2, although a handmade wig of human hair could cost between £50 and £150. "Asiatic hair is cheaper than European hair," advised *Vogue* in 1965. "The paler the hair the more expensive." Wigs were stored and styled on "Wiggy heads" and transported in cardboard wig boxes.

Wig stand **£100-120** *Wig boxes* **£200-250**

🔺 This 1964 book suggests Beatles' hair styles for female fans of the "Fab Four". London hairdressers such as Vidal Sasson and Leonard became fashionable across the world. Mary Quant and Twiggy popularized the new geometric cuts and Beatles bangs were a favourite 1960s look.

£6-12

jewellery

"The 1960s was literally a decade of swinging jewellery – long earrings dangled, chain belts encircled the waist and pendants swung from the neck." Scandinavia produced some of the most handsome designs of the period: silver and metalware pieces, abstract in design, restrained in decoration, which perfectly complemented modern styles. The teenage fashion revolution spawned a new, young look in costume jewellery. Using plastic and paper, accessories could be big and bold without being restrictively highly priced or heavy. Biba sold luminous Perspex rings as large as knuckle dusters. Sunglasses, perfect for hiding the effects of the night before, took on the dimensions of small saucers and became part of the uniform of the pop star. In the 1967 summer of love, hippies – men and women – hung flowers in their hair, love beads around their necks and bells around their ankles. But perhaps the ultimate Pop jewels were badges: cheap and throwaway, they commemorated everything from bands to protest movements while providing a minia- ture, decorative history of the period.

◄ The mid-1960s PVC bag is one of Quant's earliest handbag designs, while the acrylic pendant copies the style of her trademark five-petal daisy. The daisy symbol captured the look of the moment, but it also had a more personal significance for the designer. As a teenager she had fallen in love with an older man, who had a beautiful girlfriend. Quant was jealous and wished her dead; to her horror, her rival died suddenly of appendicitis. "I knew she was going to haunt me forever," Quant wrote. In a way she did: her name was Daisy.

Bag £300–400 *Pendant* £25–30

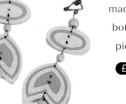

◄ Wendy Ramshaw, the celebrated British jeweller, began her career producing items in Perspex and paper that were sold through shops such as Quant's Bazaar and Way In, the trendy boutique opened on the top floor of Harrods in 1967. "Something Special" (left) dates from the same year. The paper brooches and earrings came flat-packed and were made up at home. Their value reflects both the rarity of these disposable pieces and the fame of their creator.

£500–600

➤ Plastic was the perfect medium for creating ostentatious but affordable fashion jewellery. Chunky Lucite rings in luminous colours were a favourite mod accessory. In 1966 *Vogue* featured large Perspex rings by Raymond Exton, available at the Foale and Tuffin boutique for 2½ guineas and at such stores as Biba. Similar modern rings are now on the market, so potential buyers should beware. Modern examples often have seams around the sides, whereas the originals tend to be smooth and seamless. Flowers were another popular motif, and the plastic earrings and necklace (right) provide a soft and feminine contrast to the sharp-edged geometric look.

Rings each **£18–22**   Green set **£8–12**   Orange earrings **£8–12**

🔺 These badges and patches from the late 1960s and early 1970s are devoted to diverse topics from The Beatles, Biba, drugs and sex, to Edward Heath, Che Guevara and the Vietnam War. The value of each badge depends on its subject and rarity.

Sew-on "Zap" badge **£8–10**
Set of four Beatles badges **£200–300**

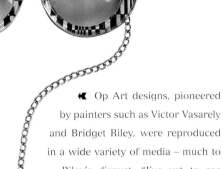

◀ Op Art designs, pioneered by painters such as Victor Vasarely and Bridget Riley, were reproduced in a wide variety of media – much to Riley's disgust. "I've yet to see an Op Art fabric which is wearable. I think they're ugly beyond belief," she confided to *Queen* magazine in 1966. These startling sunglasses can be worn, not very securely, by hanging the chains over the ears; the black-and-white discs double as pair of swinging earrings.

£10–20

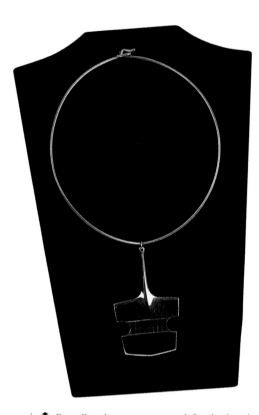

♠ Earrings varied in style during the decade from simple flower clip-ons in fabric or plastic to huge dangling creations that perfectly complemented a short geometric haircut. Light plastics and sequins ensured that earrings could be big without dragging the earlobes down to the shoulders. Chainstore pieces can still be picked up cheaply from car-boot fairs and flea markets. Designer models are more highly priced, and costume jewellery should always be checked for a maker's name or mark. These geometric triangular earrings, made from gilt and black glass, were designed by Castlecliff, USA.

£40–50

♠ Scandinavia was renowned for its hand-crafted silver and metal jewellery. Each country had its top designers, from Bjorn Weckstrom in Finland to Hans Hansen and Georg Jensen in Denmark. The silver-and-enamel choker shown above is by a Norwegian firm of silversmiths, David Anderson. Founded in 1876, the company was handed down from father to son and in the 1960s made tableware and jewellery in traditional and contemporary styles. "We view with a measure of scepticism those aspects of design which are considered high fashion and which rely for their effect on the sensational," claimed the firm somewhat primly.

£300–350

♠ The choker was a favourite 1960s shape, appearing in metal and plastic. This chrome-and-plastic set of choker and bracelet reflects Kinetic Art fashions. The circular panels contain a loose acrylic disc, which moves with the wearer.

£600–650

◀ ▲ ▶ Though traditionally catering to a more formal market, American costume jewellers learnt to swing with the times. New York designer Kenneth J. Lane experimented with new materials. The earring-and-brooch set (left) combines yellow plastic with the usual rhinestones and pearls. "In 1963 I invented costume jewellery for the beautiful people and became one of the most splendidly beautiful of them... sitting in the back of my vintage Rolls... wearing my floor-length leopard coat," remembered the jeweller, whose flamboyant creations were worn by everyone from Jackie Kennedy to musician John Cale; Cale wore a Lane choker to the Velvet Underground's debut gig. Pendants were worn by men as well as women. The gilt-and-pearl example (above left) is by the Rhode Island company Trifari. Woven with tiny glass beads, the ball necklace (above) is by American jeweller Stanley Hagler, and reflects period taste for costume jewels as big and bright as gobstoppers.

Lane set **£200–250** *Pendant* **£25–35** *Necklace* **£250–300**

♥ Traditionally small and ladylike, women's watches grew in size in the 1960s. The face of this Old England watch is large enough to cover the wrist and comes on a broad vinyl strap. Designed by Richard Loftus, Old England watches were targeted at the youth market; they were popular with both men and women. "Average prices are under £5," noted *Penthouse* magazine in 1967.

Pop watches such as this, with eye-catching fashion exteriors and cheap inner workings, tend to be ignored by serious wristwatch collectors. They are, however, sought after by 1960s style enthusiasts – hence their value.

£120–160

menswear

"One week he's in polka dots, the next week he's in stripes," sang The Kinks in 1966. Although London spearheaded the flowering of men's dress, the first "dedicated followers of fashion" were the mods in their sharp Italian suits and even sharper "winkle-pickers". As Pop styles took hold and pop stars set new trends, menswear boutiques sprang up to sell everything from guardsman's jackets to psychedelic shirts and Union Jack trousers. By the mid-1960s Carnaby Street – first colonized by designer John Stephen – was the world centre of the peacock revolution. As men grew their hair and dressed in flowers and frills, it was increasingly difficult to distinguish between the sexes. "Mothers used to cry and make their sons wear hairnets to the office," remembers designer Tommy Roberts. With the arrival of hippy fashions from the USA, men's and women's appearances became even more similar, culminating at the end of the decade in the full-blown androgyny of glam rock.

➤ Pierre Cardin designed the men's collarless jacket in 1960, but it was The Beatles who made it famous in 1963. Shown on this booklet by Pyx Publications, the look was perfect for the young band: modern enough to appeal to fans, yet respectable enough not to alienate parents. The American jacket (right) is labelled "Students Shop". The Ringo hanger by Saunders Enterprises dates from later in the 1960s, reflecting the emergence of flower power.

Hanger £15–20

Jacket £35–40   Booklet £20–30

❦ The suede jacket is by John Stephen, the "King of Carnaby Street". Stephen was only 21 when he opened his first boutique in a dingy alley off Oxford Circus in 1957. By the mid-1960s Carnaby Street was known all over the world and Stephen's men's shops had earned him the title of "the Mod Millionaire". Pop singers were among his earliest clients, and this jacket – shown with a fisherman's-style corduroy cap by Christy's, London – reflects a look sported by stars ranging from John Lennon and Bob Dylan to Donovan.

Jacket £500–550

Cap £10–15

❦ Boots were an indispensable accessory for both men and women. When Andy Warhol met Mick Jagger and David Bailey in 1963, he admired their boots from London dancewear manufacturer Anello and Davide. At first, boys had to resort either to girls' shops or to theatrical costumiers; but they soon had their own "Chelsea" boot. With elastic side gussets, pointed toes and Cuban heels, the boot was popularized by The Beatles. Also known as the "Beatle", "Beat" or "Mersey" boot, it harmonized perfectly with a pair of tight hipsters, and became a footwear classic. "Winkle-pickers", with pointed narrow toes and decorative lacings, were a favourite mod item.

£30–40 *Each pair*

➤ "We hope to stay smart for ever, not shoddy like our parents," a London mod told the *Sunday Times* in 1964. Springing from the newly affluent working class, speeding on pep pills and shiny scooters, mods (short for modernists) pioneered the peacock revolution. Their clothes ranged from Italian suits to American college styles, such as the reversible jacket on the right, teamed with tight jeans and polo shirt buttoned to the neck. A fish-tailed Parka protected these neat styles, the pockets big enough for transistors and flick-knives, as mods prepared for seaside battles with leather-jacketed, bike-riding rockers.

Shirt **£10–14**
Jacket **£100–125**

⤒ ⤳ The mid-1960s saw the adoption of a host of vintage styles, ranging from old military uniforms to Victorian frock coats. *Vogue* devoted an article to the "Attic Dress of 1965 Dandies", describing how bright young men, bored with dirty jeans, were dusting down their grandfather's clothes from the attic. "Those without attics search the markets (Portobello Road, Brixton, Church Street, Paddington). Those with the dosh… are having things made up by the sort of tailors who are amazed at nothing." High-street stores reproduced these new "old" fashions. The Kinks, loyal followers of fashion themselves, popularized the double-breasted jacket. The white jacket above left is American and labelled "Varsity Shop, L.S. Ayres and Co." The striped example in 1920s Eton boating style (above right), shown with its orginal box, is from Take Six, a successful chain of men's boutiques founded by Sidney Brent.

White jacket **£45–50** *Jacket with box* **£40–50**

⤳ Pierre Cardin dismissed ties as a bourgeois invention, and many young men dispensed with them in favour of T-shirts and turtleneck sweaters. Opulent designs remained fashionable, however. John Stephen produced flowery ties with matching shirts. London designer Mr Fish popularized and inspired the name for broad "kipper" ties; dandies sported psychedelic *foulards* with their frock coats. Even the smartest, most traditional men's stores adopted the new look: the Op Art bow tie is from the Jermyn Street emporium Turnbull & Asser.

£15–20 *Each*

➤ Psychedelic drugs and music were reflected in fashions. "Drugs are fantastically important," claimed one member of the Chelsea set. "The part they play in people's dress sense turns them on to colour." Paisley, with its swirling patterns, was popular. The floral shirt (c.1968) above typifies the romantic styles worn in the late 1960s by stars such as The Rolling Stones.

£35–45

🡅 The hippy period of the late 1960s saw the introduction of flares, bell bottoms and the appropriately named "loons". By the turn of the decade trousers had reached crazy proportions. "My trousers had enough flare to rig an East India bound clipper," remembers footballer and fashion icon George Best. Some even stitched additional fabric into their trouser bottoms. The American polyester pants above come with ready-made orange flare inserts. They are unworn (perhaps mercifully) and still have their $12.99 price tag. The frilled nylon-and-cotton shirt is also American and labelled "Delton NY".

Trousers **£20–25**   *Shirt* **£15–20**

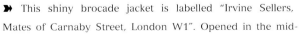

➤ This shiny brocade jacket is labelled "Irvine Sellers, Mates of Carnaby Street, London W1". Opened in the mid-1960s, Mates was one of the first boutiques to sell swinging styles to both men and women – a very profitable formula. "Sellers, at thirty, is one of the Rolls-Royce Brigade," noted fashion journalist Rodney Bennett-England in 1967. A Carnaby Street label – a symbol of 1960s cool – is still sought after by collectors.

£45–55

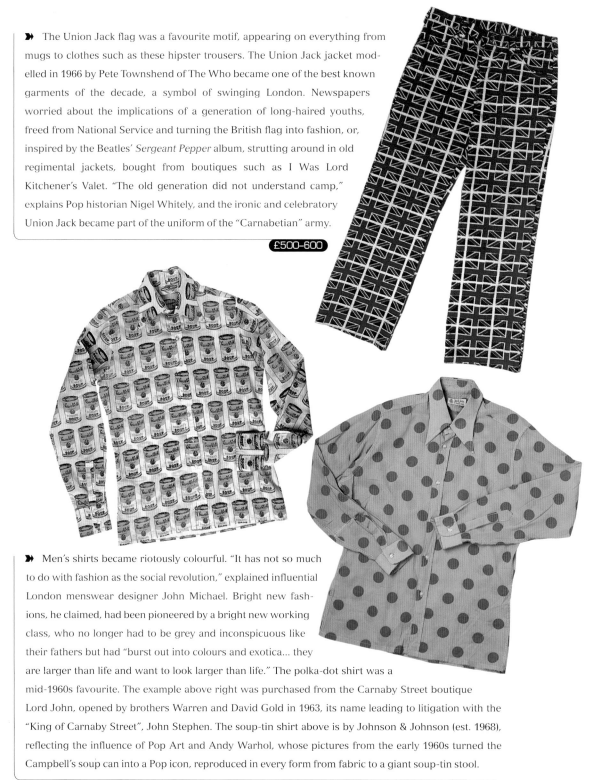

➤ The Union Jack flag was a favourite motif, appearing on everything from mugs to clothes such as these hipster trousers. The Union Jack jacket modelled in 1966 by Pete Townshend of The Who became one of the best known garments of the decade, a symbol of swinging London. Newspapers worried about the implications of a generation of long-haired youths, freed from National Service and turning the British flag into fashion, or, inspired by the Beatles' *Sergeant Pepper* album, strutting around in old regimental jackets, bought from boutiques such as I Was Lord Kitchener's Valet. "The old generation did not understand camp," explains Pop historian Nigel Whitely, and the ironic and celebratory Union Jack became part of the uniform of the "Carnabetian" army.

£500–600

➤ Men's shirts became riotously colourful. "It has not so much to do with fashion as the social revolution," explained influential London menswear designer John Michael. Bright new fashions, he claimed, had been pioneered by a bright new working class, who no longer had to be grey and inconspicuous like their fathers but had "burst out into colours and exotica... they are larger than life and want to look larger than life." The polka-dot shirt was a mid-1960s favourite. The example above right was purchased from the Carnaby Street boutique Lord John, opened by brothers Warren and David Gold in 1963, its name leading to litigation with the "King of Carnaby Street", John Stephen. The soup-tin shirt above is by Johnson & Johnson (est. 1968), reflecting the influence of Pop Art and Andy Warhol, whose pictures from the early 1960s turned the Campbell's soup can into a Pop icon, reproduced in every form from fabric to a giant soup-tin stool.

Soup-can shirt **£600–700** *Polka–dot shirt* **£25–30**

Born in Belfast in 1946, George Best joined the football team Manchester United at the age of 19 and went on to become the most celebrated footballer of his generation, renowned for his remarkable skill, his sexy looks and his wild partying. His long hair and fashionable clothes were hot news, and Best went on to open his own Manchester boutique, called Edwardia. The striped blouson jacket on the left comes from the "Best" range – and its value lies above all in its label. George Best was the first footballer to become as widely renowned as a pop star, and in true rock tradition he lived fast, played hard and, professionally at least, died young; his football career was effectively over at the age of 25.

£400–500

Men's fashions, like women's, were influenced by styles from across the world. Jackets with stand-up collars such as this example by the Scott Lester Organisation, London, reflected Indian design and were known in Britain and the USA as "Nehru" jackets after Jawaharlal Nehru, India's first prime minister. The style was popular in France, where it was named the "Mao" collar. Some fabrics and patterns were inspired by the Far East. Jackets such as the one on the right dispensed with the need for a collar and tie. They could be worn with nothing underneath or perhaps with just a turtleneck.

£300–350

Born in Deptford, south-east London, the designer Tommy Roberts became one of the in-crowd who made London swing. He opened his first shop, Kleptomania, in Carnaby Street in 1966, selling vintage clothes and Indian fashions. Moving to King's Road in 1969, Roberts launched Mr Freedom. The new boutique, patronized by everyone from The Rolling Stones to Pablo Picasso, introduced a hard-edged, pop-inspired look that was the antithesis of the soft, dreamy hippy style. The groovy jacket (c.1969) on the left is typical of Mr Freedom's bright colours and bold styling.

£350–500

London
became the style laboratory of
the world, the place where it was all
happening. Cult European directors such as
Michelangelo Antonioni and Jean-Luc Goddard set their
films in groovy, swinging London and, later, in psychedelic,
radical London. The underground scene reflected growing
disillusionment with tradition. It spawned a counter-culture
that vocalized dissent and ● invented the images of late-
20th-century life. It was a ● paradoxical decade, with the
bright Pop scene of swinging London in contrast with the
hard-edged tone of the new, gritty television dramas and
documentaries, when the message of love and peace sometimes
went missing in a drug-induced haze. But the tough-talking
journalism and hip novels, the fetishistic films and
streetwise photography remain as eminently
cool now as they ever were back in
the 1960s.

leisure

toys

For a generation of baby boomers who grew up hiding behind the sofa to watch *Dr Who* and singing "Hey Hey" with the Monkees, TV was a major influence on toys. Programmes and films all inspired their must-have merchandise, from James Bond's DB5 to the Batmobile. America led the way in providing new products for these play-ground big spenders. Barbie, the first teenage fashion doll, acquired a host of swinging imitators from Tressie to Sindy. For boys there was GI Joe (his initial popularity killed by anti-Vietnam feeling), and his more enduring English cousin, Action Man. Growing interest in nursery education inspired well-designed, constructional toys. Outdoor favourites included the Mini Moulton bike (1966), Frisbees, skateboards and the decade bounced to an end with the "Space Hopper". Children's toys were made for play but as far as collectors are concerned, value depends on condition, complete-ness and original packaging.

◄◄ Not every parent suc-cumbed to the craze for TV toys. In the UK, shops such as Galt and the cleverly named Early Learning Centre in London, stocked a select range of award-winning toys such as this cardboard doll's house. Pre-printed paper doll's houses had been made since the mid-19th century, but this example designed by Maureen Roffey A.R.C.A and manufactured by Robor Ltd., combined a historical precedent with dis-posable Pop fashion. Its ephemeral nature makes this a rare collector's item.

£400–500

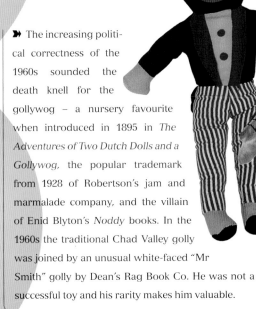

▶▶ The increasing politi-cal correctness of the 1960s sounded the death knell for the gollywog – a nursery favourite when introduced in 1895 in *The Adventures of Two Dutch Dolls and a Gollywog*, the popular trademark from 1928 of Robertson's jam and marmalade company, and the villain of Enid Blyton's *Noddy* books. In the 1960s the traditional Chad Valley golly was joined by an unusual white-faced "Mr Smith" golly by Dean's Rag Book Co. He was not a successful toy and his rarity makes him valuable.

Chad Valley golly **£25–30**   Dean's golly **£65–75**

◄◄ The "Play-plax Squares" designed by Patrick Rylands in 1965 and made by Trendon had a distinguished design history. Not only were they one of the first examples of plastic being used for quality serious play toys, but in the late 1960s the Museum of Modern Art in New York, commissioned a specially designed box in which the plastic squares were stored, like slides, at an angle, rather than laid flat as they were in the original British box. "Play-plax Squares" have since been reincarnated by Galt, but the original boxes are the collector items.

£25–35

▲ ►► The 1960s were the space-race years, with the first journeys into space at the beginning of the decade culminating with the unforgettable moment in 1969 when two astronauts – Neil Armstrong and "Buzz" Aldrin – set foot on the moon. Space technology inspired a vast number of toys, from board games with suitably evocative title and packaging to plastic and die-cast models of the various lunar space craft. Original packaging is essential.

Game **£15–25**

Model **£75–120**

▲ The "Space Hopper" was the space-age answer to the pogo stick. Distributed by Mettoy, the "amazing inflatable riding ball" was made in blue (now rare) or orange vinyl; it came flat packed in a box (even rarer) and had to be inflated with a bicycle pump. Few examples have survived in good condition after hours of bouncing or proximity to radiators or fires.

£35–45

➤ Trolls were one of the more bizarre sixties crazes. The troll was a figure from Scandinavian mythology and the most collectable examples were manufactured by Dam Things in Denmark. Thomas Dam carved large wooden trolls for funfairs. These proved so successful that his family produced troll dolls made from natural rubber and filled with wood shavings, with hand-made felt clothes and real sheepskin hair. Trolls were an international success and launched in Britain in 1964, promoted by the unlikely figure of Diana Dors. The giraffe and the large troll are stamped with the Dam logo on the foot.

Large troll **£75–85** *Small troll* **£20–30** *Giraffe troll* **£80–100**

❦ In order to compete with teenage fashion dolls, traditional baby dolls had to develop some new tricks. Launched by Palitoy in 1966, Tiny Tears was a best-seller. When fed with a bottle of water, not only did she wet herself, but she could also cry real tears. This version comes in a box that opens to form a baby bath.

£40–45

♠ Rich, glamorous and beautiful, "Barbie", the first teenage fashion doll, was also a barometer of American culture from her launch in 1959 by Mattel. In spite of her blonde hair, this "Barbie", with her sophisticated hairstyle and pink couture evening gown, was influenced by Jackie Kennedy whose reign as fashion icon outlived her tragically short stay in the White House. Blonde "Barbies" far outnumber their brunette and redheaded sisters and are therefore less valuable. Any "Barbie" will need all her accessories, original packaging and, ideally, be in mint condition, for top value.

£80–100

◄ ↟ Inspired by the success of Mattel's "Barbie", in 1962 Pedigree launched the British "Sindy". She enjoyed an equally enviable lifestyle with a host of designer outfits, friends (she was joined by her boyfriend, Paul, in 1965) and consumer goods, including the record player shown here, which was the essential accessory for any 1960s teenager. "Sindy" was promoted as "the doll you love to dress"; her "Weekenders" outfit seen here, in which she made her television debut in 1963, was created by Foale & Tuffin, whose trendy clothes were modelled by Twiggy and sold in Carnaby Street.

Sindy £130–160   Record player £14–16

"Sindy... the doll you love to dress"

➤ "Action Man", based on Hasbro's "GI Joe" – the first boy's doll – with his scarred cheek, was the ultimate would-be macho role model, who truly caught the imagination of those too young to fear the Vietnam War and the draft. The first British "Action Man" was made under licence by Palitoy from 1966, although it was marked with a copyright date of 1964. The earlier, more collectable "Action Soldier", shown here, has pinned metal wrist joints and moulded, painted hair. He will be twice as valuable if he still has his original box and accessories, especially his hat and identity tag.

£80–100

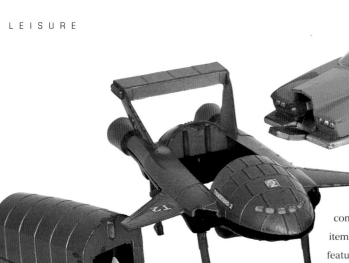

Gerry Anderson's supermarionation was the success story of children's television in the 1960s. Programmes such as *Stingray*, *Fireball XL5*, *Captain Scarlet and the Mysterions* and *Thunderbirds* had children (and adults) glued to the set and inspired toys, comics, books and records that are now cult collector items. *Thunderbirds* – the first, hour-long puppet film series, featuring 20in- (51cm-) high puppets – was launched in 1965; the feature film *Thunderbirds are Go!*, which included songs performed by the puppet Cliff Richard Jr & the Shadows, followed in 1966. In 1967 Dinky were licensed to produce the "Thunderbird 2" freighter spacecraft, with spring-operated extending legs, which carried the yellow "Thunderbird 4", an underwater craft, in a detachable pod; on land, Lady Penelope, chauffered by Parker, played her part as an International Rescue agent in her pink six-wheeled Rolls Royce "FAB 1".

Thunderbirds 2 & 4 (boxed) £100–200

Rolls Royce (boxed) £200–220

Records (each) £30–50

The fortunes of the English firm Corgi were transformed in the 1960s, when the company issued a gift set of the cars from another home-grown cult television series, *The Avengers*. Launched in 1961, the hero Steed, the archetypal English dandy with a Vintage Bentley to match, was accompanied by a succession of beautiful and intrepid female assistants, among them Mrs Catherine Gale (Honor Blackman) in a black leather catsuit and high boots. From 1965, Steed was joined by Emma Peel (played by Diana Rigg), in equally figure-hugging stretch jersey and driving a sporty white Lotus Elan S2.

£180–200

Cars remained the ultimate status symbol, and no self-respecting hero of the small or large screen or the comic book was without a distinctive model, often with bizarre personal modifications. From 1966, Batman and Robin countered the forces of evil in colour on television in their Batmobile, which was produced as a diecast by Corgi. The urbane Simon Templar, the "Robin Hood of crime" and hero of Leslie Charteris's *Saint* books, was played in the TV series launched in 1963 by Roger Moore. Templar operated from a more discreet, yellow, two-seater sports Volvo P1800, which was produced as a diecast. Both cars are eagerly sought by collectors but unboxed and battered they are worth less than £5 each.

Boxed, each **£200–220**

"Exterminate, exterminate" was the spine-chilling cry of the Daleks: the real stars of the BBC *Dr Who* television series, launched in 1963. Toy daleks with battery-operated swivel movements were produced in moulded plastic under licence by the American company Marx in the 1960s and Palitoy in the 1970s. Thanks to repeat showings and a cult following, production has restarted using the original tooling. However, Daleks made in the 1960s and still with their original packaging are the ones to look out for.

£140–160

The Man from U.N.C.L.E, American television's answer to the James Bond films, ran from 1964 until 1968 and was shown in 62 countries. It starred Super Agents Napoleon Solo (Robert Vaughn) and Illya Kuryakin (David McCallum) from the United Network for Law Enforcement. Their mission in life was to bust the international crime syndicate, Thrush. Corgi's Man from U.N.C.L.E Thrush-Buster (1966) was produced both in blue and the rarer white. Boxed examples should include the Waverly ring.

£90–150

117

rock and pop

Just as The Beatles dominated music in the 1960s, so they remain top of the "all-time greats" list and of the international market for rock and pop memorabilia today. Record prices are regularly paid at sales of Beatles-related items and this has been the case since such auctions began at the start of the 1980s. The 1960s are often described as rock's golden age, and demand for all material from this period is particularly strong. The market offers the collector a great diversity of memorabilia at all price levels. Records – including demonstration discs, known as demos, and EPs (7 inch singles) – are a major collecting field. Many of them are still modestly priced, but there are also instruments, autographed items, clothing, posters, merchandise and stars' personal effects and awards. Links with a legendary name, such as John Lennon, can transform an everyday object into a very valuable collectable.

◀◀ Beatles' autographs are highly sought after but they have also been the most faked, both in the sixties and more recently. If this photograph, which purports to be a 1960s image with a 1990s signature were genuine it would be worth £150. As a forgery it is valueless. Items should be supported by a guarantee and checked by a specialist.

£0

❧ Manufacturers in the UK and USA wasted little time in cashing in on Beatlemania from the early 1960s, producing an enormous range of merchandise for the teenage fan. Wares included clothing, furnishings, school equipment, toiletries, games, dolls and even confectionery. Most of it was expensive, and some products, such as the inflatable dolls shown below, were certainly kitsch. As the result of poor business deals, the Beatles themselves made very little from this phenomenon.

£80–120

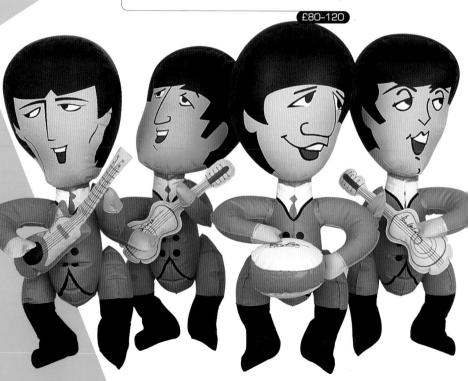

➤ The Beatles made several recordings in Hamburg in 1961 and 1962 with singer Tony Sheridan, including the EP, shown far right, which was released in 1964. First pressings of their number-one album *Please Please Me* have black labels with gold lettering. A stereo copy in excellent condition can be worth £1000 and above; mono copies are much less valuable. Most Beatles' Parlophone singles were available to disc-jockeys as demos, or demonstration records, first with red and white and later green and white "A" labels; all are very desirable.

Left £350–400   *Centre* £350–450
Right £100–150

❮ A range of jewellery was produced as part of the wave of merchandise that resulted from the huge success of The Beatles. All pieces featured the likenesses of the "Fab Four", usually in a simplistic representation, and most had facsimile signatures either on the item itself or on the backing card, as shown with this guitar brooch. In common with all other examples of 1960s Beatles merchandise, items that are in top condition, and still accompanied by their original packaging, are most sought after by collectors.

Left £15–20   *Right* £8–10

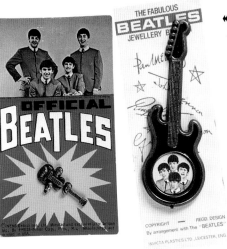

➤ Widely regarded as *the* rock album of all time, The Beatles' *Sergeant Pepper's Lonely Hearts Club Band* also broke new ground in the design of its cover – the work of artist Peter Blake. The album's release on 1 June 1967 helped to set the tone for the so-called "summer of love". The psychedelic theme continued with the single *Magical Mystery Tour*, released in December 1967. The first pressings of the EP contain a blue booklet/lyric sheet insert.

Sgt Pepper £30–50   *Magical Mystery Tour* £25–30

◖◖ "Would you let your daughter marry a Rolling Stone?" asked the press. The Stones strutted into the charts with the 1963 Decca single *Come On* (demo shown). The 1967 album *Their Satanic Majesties Request* (far left), with its three-dimensional cover, coincided with drugs busts and court cases. *Street Fighting Man* caught the mood of the turbulent late 1960s; this rare picture sleeve was banned in the UK. Brian Jones's death in 1969 was for many the end of the 1960s dream.

Album ⬤£50–60⬤   Demo ⬤£50–70⬤   Single ⬤£100–120⬤

▶▶ The Small Faces made some of the most innovative pop records of the decade. Their sharp mod image, seen on their second LP *From the Beginning* (1967), became psychedelic. *Itchycoo Park* (demo, far right) introduced the spacey musical effect of phasing. The sleeve of *Ogden's Nut Gone Flake* (1968) alludes to "going off your nut smoking weed". Collectors need to keep a clear head, however, since this album was reissued in the 1970s.

Left ⬤£60–70⬤   Centre ⬤£70–80⬤   Right ⬤£40–50⬤

"Going off your nut smoking weed"

♥ When Rhythm and Blues (R&B) clubs sprang up in London, the Artwoods and Zoot Money's Big Roll Band were both popular live acts, but never achieved big record sales, hence the rarity of these two 1966 EPs. Like the Stones, the Yard Birds' fame transcended the hip R&B circuit partly thanks to guitar heroes Eric Clapton, and later Jimmy Page and Jeff Beck, who both play on the 1966 demo (centre) *Happening Ten Years Time Ago*.

Left ⬤£250–300⬤   Centre ⬤£40–50⬤   Right ⬤£300–350⬤

◀◀ These two puppets, by well-known British makers Pelham, embody changing pop fashions of the decade. The early Beatles model (far left) has a mop-top wig, Pierre Cardin-style suit, and a very McCartneyesque face. Pelham lacked a licence to make official Beatles merchandise, so their "Pop Singers" range featured a guitarist, drummer and un-Fab Four saxophonist. Like many real-life 1960s rock stars, the later puppet (near left) has grown his hair and swapped suit and tie for purple flares and psychedelic shirt. These figures reflect children's new-found fascination with pop in the wake of Beatlemania – as shown by the appearance of pop groups on the children's show *Blue Peter* and a performance by a group of puppets called Cliff Richard Jr & The Shadows in the 1966 *Thunderbirds Are Go* movie. Acts such as The Monkees were targeted partly at children, and spawned their own merchandise, from dolls to cars.

"Beatle" £80–100

Psychedelic £65–100

➤➤ "I hope I die before I get old," sang Roger Daltrey on the album *My Generation* in 1965, a wish that was tragically fulfilled by many pop stars, including The Who's own drummer, Keith Moon. The Who released their first single *I'm the Face"/"Zoot Suit* in 1964 under the name High Numbers. A rare second issue, with *Zoot* on the A side, is shown top right. As The Who, they reached their mod audience to become the band that encapsulated youthful frustration – epitomized by Pete Townshend's signature destruction of his guitar. Early Who demos are collectable, and the 1965 demo single *La-la-la-lies* (bottom right) could be worth up to twice as much as indicated if accompanied by its picture sleeve.

Album £70–100   *"Zoot Suit"* £350–400   *Demo* £100–125

➤ The Kinks's string of hits, including the 1964 EP shown right, helped to popularize the "dandy" look typified by high-collared jackets and frilly shirts. Their classic song *Waterloo Sunset* reached number four in 1967, the same year that the group The Move released their third hit, *Flowers in the Rain*. This single, which captured the spirit of the time, has the distinction of being the very first record broadcast on Radio 1 when the station went on air, on 30 September. The example shown is the actual demonstration copy that was played.

The Move **£30–40**   *The Kinks* **£25–35**

◀ Radio Luxembourg – one of the first stations to cater for the new audience of pop fans in Europe and the UK – was a pioneer in a medium that had previously concentrated on programming for the older generation. The growing youth market also led to the emergence of "pirate" radio stations, so-called because they were unlicensed and broadcast from ships off the British coast. The BBC eventually responded by launching Radio 1, using many former "pirate" disc-jockeys.

£5–10   *Each*

➤ David Bowie (b.1947 as David Robert Jones) began his career with a number of obscure singles produced under various guises. In 1964, as David Jones & The King Bees, he recorded *Liza Jane* and *Louie, Louie Go Home* on the Vocalion label, of which a demonstration copy is shown bottom right. He also had little success with his 1967 and 1969 self-titled albums. All that changed with the release of the 1969 single *Space Oddity*, coinciding as it did with the attention on space exploration generated by the first moon landing, by American astronauts Neil Armstrong (b.1930) and "Buzz" Aldrin (b.1930) in the Apollo 11 on 20 July 1969.

Left **£200–300**   *Centre* **£400–700**   *Right* **£125–175**

◀◀ Like David Bowie, Marc Bolan had several attempts at stardom. *The Third Degree* (left), his second single for Decca, was issued in 1966. He then joined the group John's Children; some copies of their 1967 single (bottom left) were sold in a picture sleeve. After forming the duo Tyrannosaurus Rex – a demo of whose *By the Light of the Magical Moon* is shown bottom right – Bolan hit number one with the renamed T.Rex in 1970. His success continued into the 1970s – the 1971 preview single top left was a free concert handout to promote the *Electric Warrior* album.

Preview single	£175–220	*Third Degree*	£300–350
John's Children	£75–100	*Magical Moon*	£100–150

"Je T'Aime Moi Non Plus" was widely banned from radio playlists

🔺 The early 1960s saw the rise of British female stars. Sixteen-year-old Helen Shapiro toured with the relatively unknown Beatles in Spring 1963. Fellow Liverpudlian Priscilla White changed her name to Cilla Black and had her first hit, *Love of the Loved*, written by Lennon and McCartney. In 1964, 14-year-old Lulu burst onto the scene with *Shout*, while Marianne Faithfull also made the charts with her debut single, the Jagger and Richards composition *As Tears Go By*. Brigitte Bardot (b.1934), the 1960s answer to Marilyn Monroe (1926–62), didn't need a singing career but still released an album in 1963. In the late 1960s, Jane Birkin and Serge Gainsbourg gained notoriety with their sexually explicit song *Je T'Aime Moi Non Plus*, which was widely banned from playlists.

Far left	£15–35	*Top left*	£12–15	*Bottom left*	£15–25
Centre	£30–40	*Bottom right*	£50–70	*Right*	£20–30

➤ The American singer Bob Dylan (b.1941) was the antithesis of the traditional pop star. His albums, including *Bringing It All Back Home* (1965), whose songbook is shown right, proved that there could be more to pop music than the catchy, three-minute love song. His influence can be heard on such albums as *What's Bin Did And What's Bin Hid* (1965) by Donovan, who was dubbed the "English Bob Dylan".

Donovan **£15–25**   Dylan **£25–35**

◄◄ One response of the American music scene to the British "invasion" of 1964 and 1965 was to promote Soul and Rhythm and Blues (R & B) labels such as Detroit's Tamla Motown, whose stable of acts included The Supremes and The Four Tops. The label dominated black music throughout the decade, notching up many international hits. After fronting The Supremes, Diana Ross went solo and continued to enjoy superstar status in the 1970s. Martha Reeves & The Vandellas' 1964 hit *Dancing in the Street* was successfully covered by David Bowie and Mick Jagger, reaching number one in the British charts in 1985.

Top left **£10–15**   Bottom left **£70–100**
Top right **£30–50**   Bottom right **£70–100**

➤ Millie's 1964 single *My Boy Lollipop* was probably the first UK hit with a reggae beat. Many copies of her first release, the 1961 EP *Millie*, on the Blue Beat label, were issued without a sleeve; illustrated on the far right is one of the rare examples *with* its cover. The first two recordings made by Bob Marley (1945–81) were both released in 1963 under the name Robert Marley. His second recording, featured near right, was *One Cup of Coffee*, the B-side of which was the song *Exodus* by Ernest Ranglin.

One Cup of Coffee **£175–225**
Millie **£130–160**

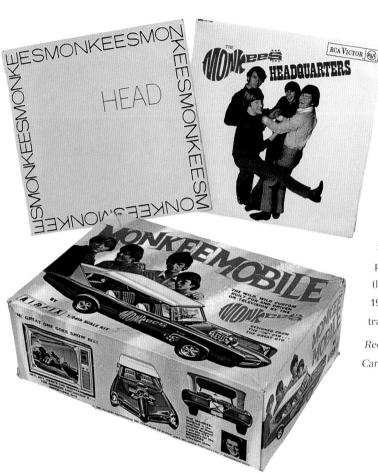

The Monkees could be regarded as the first "boy band", put together so as to appeal specifically to adolescent girls. The formula worked and, with a run of hits and a television series on both sides of the Atlantic, they were among the biggest names in pop music – despite rumours that they never actually performed on their recordings. Their success prompted a rash of merchandise similar to that seen in the case of The Beatles, including a plastic model kit of the "Monkeemobile" (left). The LP *Headquarters* came out in 1967. The group's last album , a film soundtrack called *Head,* was released in 1969.

Records: Left **£50–60** Right **£10–15**
Car **£150–200**

The Monkees were the first "boy band"

While Britain was in the grip of Beatlemania, the USA had its own new craze in the form of "surf" music, originating in California, with songs based on high-school obsessions: surfing, dating and hot-rod cars. Albums such as *All Summer Long* and singles including *Help Me Rhonda* established The Beach Boys as the undisputed leaders of the pack. A demonstration version of the latter is shown bottom right. In 1966 their music became more serious; and their album *Pet Sounds* was admired by The Beatles. Other "surf" artists included Dick Dale, who in 1963 styled himself as "King of the Surf Guitar".

Dick Dale **£35–55**

Beach Boys Single **£15–25** Beach Boys Album **£12–18**

➤ The breathtaking guitar technique and flamboyant dress-sense of rock icon Jimi Hendrix (1942–70) was a potent combination. Arriving in London in 1966, Hendrix soon drew the respect of many stars, including Eric Clapton (b.1945) and Pete Townshend of The Who. Certainly a legend in his lifetime, Jimi's premature death in September 1970 ensured his status as a rock icon, and he is now one of the most collectable names in the memorabilia market. His trademark black hat, featured above – seen on the cover of the 1968 album *Smash Hits* – was sold in a London auction in 1991 for £14,300. In his short career Hendrix released only a handful of albums. His second was *Axis: Bold As Love* (1967), an example of which is shown right.

Hat **£15000+** *Album* **£40–180**

❰ Pink Floyd were one of the first groups to introduce British audiences to concert light-show techniques developed on the West Coast of the USA. Their live performances became legendary, and their long instrumental pieces had a crucial influence on a new wave of groups. Illustrated near left is a very rare picture-sleeve demonstration version of their second single, *See Emily Play* (1967), which was first aired on BBC Radio 1. The other record is a French issue of their first LP, *Piper at the Gates of Dawn*. A British first mono pressing of this album can be worth up to £150.

Album **£35–40** *Single* **£300–500**

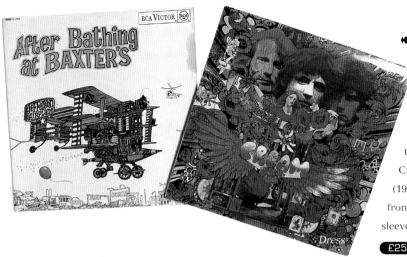

Jefferson Airplane's first two albums, released in 1967 and 1968 – the second of which, *After Bathing At Baxter's* is shown (left) in first issue – were released with black labels and are worth two or three times more than repressings with orange labels. Cream's eye-catching LP *Disraeli Gears* (1967) was issued with a sleeve laminated front and back; 1968 copies came with a sleeve laminated only on the front.

£25–35 *Each*

Led Zeppelin had no commercially released singles. Several were produced but later withdrawn or produced as promotional copies only. Any examples are therefore highly desirable. The group's success was based solely on LP releases and concerts. Their first, eponymous LP, issued in 1969, contained a dazzling and pioneering fusion of heavy rock, blues and folk. First pressings, such as the example below, are distinguished by turquoise lettering on the front; second pressings feature orange lettering and are worth up to approximately £18. The group's career was brought to a sudden end by the death of drummer John Bonham in 1980.

£100-150

"Woodstock: perhaps the last great expression of the 1960s philosophy of love and peace."

As the decade drew to a close, the Woodstock Music & Arts Fair in August 1969 could be seen as perhaps the last great expression of the 1960s philosophy of love and peace. One manifestation of this great ideal had been the phenomenon of the open-air music festival, often staged over several days. Held in New York State, Woodstock attracted an audience of some 400,000 people to listen to such outstanding artists as Jimi Hendrix. These trousers are extremely rare and they represent a record of one of the most famous rock concerts of all times.

£400-600

127

film and tv

In the 1960s film actresses began to bare all. Jane Fonda, Vanessa Redgrave and Catherine Deneuve, following the example of Brigitte Bardot, starred in erotic roles. Meanwhile, Audrey Hepburn did for the gamine look in the cinema what Twiggy was doing in fashion. Men stayed macho, whether it was Sean Connery in the early Bond movies or the irresistible Marcello Mastroianni in numerous Italian art films. Italy was a big influence, just as much as in fashion and interiors, with Italians, Federico Fellini and Michelangelo Antonioni making modern classics such as *La Dolce Vita* and *Blow-Up*. British film and television reflected a grittier urban realism, with hugely influential documentaries such as *Cathy Come Home* and plays including Nell Dunn's *Up the Junction* dealing with social issues and working-class life. This was when the BBC established itself as a producer of quality television, bringing out long-running British classics as *Steptoe and Son*, *Dad's Army*, *Tomorrow's World* and *Top of the Pops*.

◄◄ Federico Fellini's *La Dolce Vita* (1960) has American beauty Anita Ekberg pursued by admirer Marcello Mastroianni, as the gossip columnist trying to make it as a writer but encountering trouble wherever he goes. The film's revelations about Roman high society, some of whom appeared in *La Dolce Vita*, caused a scandal when it was released, with the Vatican very hostile to it. *La Dolce Vita* introduced the word "paparazzo".

£3500–4000

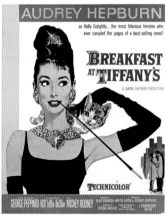

▲ "I never try to scandalise people, but they sometimes scandalise themselves", said director Luis Buñuel about *Belle de Jour* (1966). The film starred Catherine Deneuve as a housewife whose masochistic daydreams mingle with her daily life. Deneuve's jaded, amoral glamour contrasted with the tomboy-girl image of the elegant star, Audrey Hepburn, who as Holly Golightly in *Breakfast at Tiffany's* (1961) shows "a fey, comic talent that should enchant".

Belle de Jour poster £3000–3500

Breakfast at Tiffany's poster £1500–2000

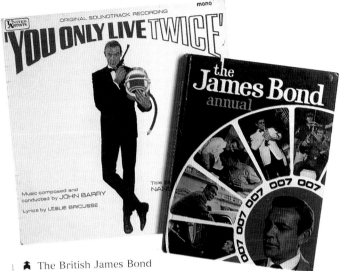

▲ The British James Bond films, based on Ian Fleming's best-selling original novels, created the unforgettable tough-guy we still love to watch, played in the early years by Sean Connery. The spin-off merchandise linked to the films, such as the United Artists long-play album *You Only Live Twice* and the James Bond annual shown here, is very desirable.

Album £25–30   *Annual* £8–10

➤ These Pan paperbacks reflect a new wave of social realist films and televison programmes concentrating on working people's lives. Jeremy Sandford's BBC drama, *Cathy Come Home* focused on homelessness and inspired the foundation of the charity Shelter. Nell Dunn's *Up the Junction,* set among South London housing estates, was shown as part of the BBC's risk-taking "Wednesday Play" series, which dealt with such controversial left of centre social issues as abortion. Julie Christie starred in Richard Lester's 1968 film *Petulia* about a socialite's adulterous affair.

Each £4–6

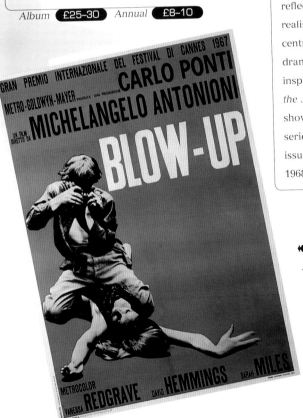

◄ More than any other film of the decade Michelangelo Antonioni's *Blow-Up* (1967), made for Metro-Goldwyn Meyer, caught the decadent, anarchic mood. David Hemmings is a fashion photographer who accidentally snaps a murder in a London park – or has he imagined it? The film sneaked past the censors despite two teenage girls – one of them Jane Birkin – taking off their clothes. The film poster is as ambiguously sexy as the film itself.

£300–400

➤ How to make your own pet snake: collect several toilet rolls, paint them, thread a piece of handy string right through and add sellotape – "I mean sticky tape" – and of course, sticky back plastic. Or something along those lines. The 41-year-old children's TV show *Blue Peter* is famous for its theme tune, pets, appeals, expeditions and model-making. "Here's one I made earlier", was the catchphrase of Chris Trace and Valerie Singleton, shown here on the cover of the very first *Blue Peter Annual* (1964), with Petra the dog.

£130–180

BBC tv
The book which five million young viewers have been waiting for!
Blue Peter
The features and personalities of your favourite television programme

◄◄ Classic cartoons *Yogi Bear, The Flintstones* and *The Jetsons* were created by the partnership of Americans William Hanna and Joseph Barbera. *The Flintstones*, an irresistible story of a stone-age family, was the first prime-time cartoon made for television – the original episodes hit the small screen in 1960. The catchy, cult theme-tunes were composed by veteran tunester Hoyt Curtain, and the records featuring his inimitable tunes are highly collectable.

The Flintstones and Yogi Bear **£15–20** Each

The Jetsons **£20–25**

➤ Many of the BBC's top shows had their first airing in the 1960s, including *Tomorrow's World* and *Top of the Pops*. Also notable was *Z-Cars*: a compelling drama about the everyday lives of earthy Northern policemen, who drank and bet on horses. The series ran from 1962 to 1978 and signalled the BBC's commitment to serious drama. ITV's *Emergency Ward 10*, set in Oxbridge General Hospital, was a successful twice-weekly soap depicting the lives of doctors, nurses and patients. It featured the first inter-racial kiss on British television. The annual and tea towel give a flavour of the two series.

Annual **£15–20** *Tea Towel* **£8–10**

◀◀ In the 1960s, the rock film came into its own. The Beatles brought out an animated cartoon, *Yellow Submarine*, which was directed by George Dunning and scripted by Lee Minoff. John, Paul, George and Ringo became cartoon characters wandering through a psychedelic universe in search of "Pepperland" and hotly pursued by the "Blue Meanies". Merchandise from the film, including this 1969 Corgi model of the submarine, is now very much in demand. The poster beneath advertises D.A. Pennebaker's documentary film of Bob Dylan's 1965 tour of the UK, when he was accompanied by Joan Baez and Alan Price. Pennebaker's work set the standard and style for a host of rock documentaries made since, from *Woodstock* to *This is Spinal Tap*.

Model Yellow Submarine £250–350
Bob Dylan poster £400–500

▶▶ *Barbarella* (1968) made by French director Roger Vadim and starring his then wife, Jane Fonda alongside such canonic sixties actors as David Hemmings and Anita Pallenberg, was a bizarre piece of futuristic erotica. Vadim had already launched a previous wife, Brigitte Bardot, as a sex-goddess, and *Barbarella,* inspired by Jean-Claude Forest's notoriously risqué comic-strip, did the same for Fonda. Barbarella rescues the 40th century from destruction, frequently appearing nude or scantily clad.

£600–800

131

books and mags

"Is it a book you would wish your wife or servant to read?" thundered the prosecutor at the infamous Lady Chatterley trail in 1960. Clearly the answer was yes. The jury found Penguin not guilty of obscenity. D.H.Lawrence's uncensored novel sold 200,000 copies on the first day of publication and this literary event set the tone of the sixties. "Sexual intercourse began in 1963..." wrote poet Philip Larkin, "Between the end of the Chatterley ban and the Beatles' first LP." A new generation of "Angry Young Writers" charted the impact of changing social and sexual mores. The Cold War inspired a wealth of spy novels, whilst reaction against the Vietnam War and the burgeoning hippy movement stimulated psychedelic prose and protest poetry. But the most flourishing form of literature in this disposable decade was magazines: from *Private Eye* (launched 1961) to the Sunday colour supplements to the Underground press.

◄◄ John Le Carré's seminal spy novel inaugurated a new type of spy thriller, which was more realistic than Ian Fleming's James Bond. *The Spy who came in from the Cold*, shown here in first edition, caught the complicated mood of Cold War espionage: double agents and double dealing with a whiff of romance.

£300–500

❦ "Kitchen Sink" or "Angries" were descriptions loosely applied to a selection of writers who focused on working-class settings and explored the social revolution. For female characters, the price of sexual liberation was invariably pregnancy. Lynne Reid Banks's heroine retreats to her L-shaped room in a squalid Fulham boarding house to hide her shame, but discovers a new independence. Bill Naughton's Alfie, with his "Tonik" suit by Dormeuil and his Ford Consul is a modern-day working class Casanova out for what he can get.

The L-Shaped Room **£20–30** *Alfie* **£40–55**

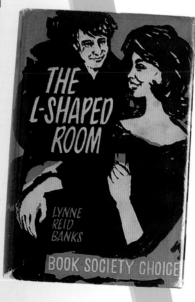

◀◀ Joseph Heller's famous anti-war novel introduced a new catchprase to the language. For Captain Yossarian, World War II pilot, the only way to avoid death was to ask to be grounded because of insanity. But if you were rational enough to ask, then you couldn't be crazy – hence the Catch 22 of the title. This first US edition (1961) is inscribed, signed and dated by its reclusive author, hence its value.

£1500–2200

▶▶ Anthony Burgess's *A Clockwork Orange* was the original novel that became Stanley Kubrick's shocking film starring Malcolm McDowell as the disaffected Alex. The novel, shown here in a rare proof edition, had a more religious slant than the film and was intended by Burgess as a piece of "high Modernism" like the work of James Joyce. Like Joyce's books, *A Clockwork Orange* mounts a devastating attack on the hypocrisy of the Establishment.

£950–1500

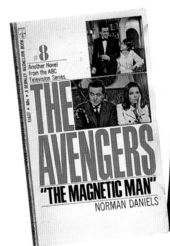

▲ It was typical of "youthquake", that in 1966 when London was at its most swinging, Mary Quant published her autobiography at the age of 32. Told at top speed, in the slang of the day ("birds", "groovy gear"), it provides a fascinating portrayal of Quant and the Chelsea Look. The book includes pictures of her original designs.

£15–25

▲ Paperbacks began to take over from hardbacks in the 1960s, pulp and detective fiction proving best-sellers. These books celebrate two cult TV series and though still inexpensive, this style of book, with their period photographic covers, is collectable.

£5–8 *Each*

❧ The development of London as the new fashion capital spawned a host of influential magazines. "When did you last hear the word austerity?"demanded *The Queen* magazine in 1959. "This is the age of Boom." *Queen* dropped its old-fashioned "the" and itself became a symbol of sixties boom with top photographs and popular features. *Nova*, launched 1965, was "a new kind of magazine for a new kind of woman", and as well as innovative design and fashion, was among the first woman's journal to cover sex. *Boutique*, poppy and gossipy, was a forerunner of *Hello*.

Queen **£7–15**   Nova **£10–15**   Boutique **£10–15**

➤ The Underground press mushroomed magically in the 1960s, catering for the hippies, the freaks and the new "alternative lifestyle". *International Times* (1966) was one of the most prominent radical rags, its offices regularly raided by the police who removed everything in the hope of finding incriminating evidence. "Its attitudes are totally predicatable," commented George Melly. "It's in favour of soft drugs, free love, screwing the system, avant-garde Pop..." *Gandalf's Garden*, inspired by Tolkien's *Lord of the Rings* (the hippy bible), and targeted at "the flying saucer set" only lasted three issues. Nevertheless it is an example of the transient but perfect blossom of flower-power publishing.

Gandalf's Garden **£100–150**

The International Times **£10–40**

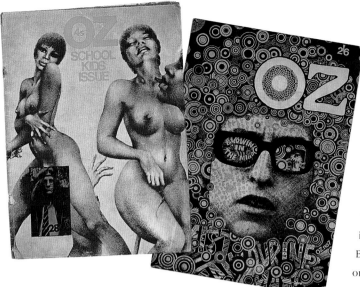

◀◀ Founded by Australian Richard Neville in Sydney in 1963, and launched in Britain in 1967, *OZ* became the most famous Underground magazine. Articles ranged from Germaine Greer writing about groupies, to a users' guide to LSD, although the innovative, psychedelic design made much of the writing illegible. The notorious "Schoolkids" issue (1970) included a cartoon of Rupert Bear that resulted in the editors being put on trial, a celebrated clash between the hippy Underground and the Establishment.

"Schoolkids" **£100–150**

Issue no.7 **£50–80**

🏹 Paperback books were a favourite Underground medium. Created by Peter Max, psychedelic designer and self-confessed "Champion of Love", *The Paper Airplane Book* (1971) contains D.I.Y paper planes in the "aerodynamic colours of love" designed to be thrown at rock concerts. The cover of the central book (modern poetry from *Breakthru International Poetry Magazine*, Corgi, 1968) is designed by Hapshash and the Coloured Coat. *Alternative London*, signed by author Nicholas Saunders (1970) has a black and white Op Art cover and provides a hippy guide to London.

Paper Airplane **£200–250** *Others (each)* **£30–50**

🏹 Increased prosperity led to a growing number of interiors magazines showing the latest looks in homes and furnishings. These provide an invaluable reference tool to the period and are sought after by dealers and collectors. Look out too, for period store catalogues such as Biba and Habitat.

£10–12

135

useful addresses

Where to buy

The following shops and antiques dealers offer a range of collectable items dating from the 1960s. Markets and fairs are also good hunting grounds.

Dealers

Alfie's Antiques Market
13–25 Church Street
London NW8 8DT

At Alfies
Antigo *Decorative arts*
Circle *Decorative arts*
Collector's World *Toys*
Richard Gibbon *Costume Jewellery*
Glassworks *Italian glass*
David Huxtable *Tins, ephemera and packaging*
Francesca Martine *Jewellery and decorative arts*
John Rastall *Ceramics and decorative arts*
Persiflage *Women's fashions, accessories, lingerie and swimwear*
Sparkle Moore *Fashions and household items*
Alvin Ross *Toys*

Beatcity
PO Box 229 Chatham
Kent ME5 0PW
01634 844525 or 0370 650890

Boom!
53 Chalk Farm Road
Camden, London NW1 8AN
020 7284 4622
Furniture, technology and decorative arts

Chelsea Clocks
Stand H3–4 R1–2 Antiquarius
131–141 King's Road, London SW3
Clocks

Childhood Memories
The Farnham Antique Centre
27 South Street, Farnham
Surrey GU9 7QU
01252 724475/793704

Delta of Venus
(contact c/o Leigh Wildman)
151 Drummond Street
London NW1 2PB
020 7387 3037
Decorative arts and household wares

Flying Duck Enterprises
320–322 Creek Road, London SE10
020 8858 1964
Decorative arts and household wares

The Ginnel Gallery
18–22 Lloyd Street
Manchester M2 5WA
0161 833 9037
Decorative arts

Memory Lane Records
(contact Mike Reynolds)
55 Frith Road, Croydon CR0 1TB
020 8649 7220
Vintage records and books on music

Modern Age Vintage Clothing
65 Chalk Farm Road
London NW1
020 7482 3787
Fashions

On the Air
42 Bridge Street Row
Chester CH1 1NN
01244 348 468
Portable radios

Planet Bazaar
151 Drummond Street
London NW1 2PB
020 7387 8326
Decorative arts

Radio Days
87 Lower Marsh, London SE1 7AB
020 7928 0800
Fashion and accessories

The Reel Poster Company
72 Westbourne Grove
London W2 5SH
020 7727 4488
Film posters

Rennies

13 Rugby Street

London WC1 3QT

020 7405 0220

Decorative arts

Rokit

225 Camden High Street

London NW1

020 7267 3046

and at 23 Kensington Gardens

Brighton, East Sussex

Vintage clothing

Steinberg & Tolkien

193 King's Road

London SW3

020 7376 3660

Designer fashions and accessories

Target Gallery

7 Windmill Street

London W1P 1HF

020 7636 6295

Furniture, decorative arts,

books and posters

Tom Tom

42 New Compton St

London WC2

020 7240 7909

Post-war design and decorative arts

Twenty Twenty One

(Simon Alderson/Tony Cummings)

274 Upper St, London N1 2UA

020 7288 1996

Furniture, design and decorative arts

Nigel Williams

22 & 25 Cecil Court

London WC2N 4HE

020 7836 7757

Vintage books

Zambesi

The Old Horse Hospital

Stables Market, Chalk Farm Road

London NW1

Street Markets

Camden Market

Chalk Farm Road

London NW1

Open Saturday & Sunday

Portobello Market

Portobello Road

London W11

Open Friday & Saturday

Auction Houses

Bonhams, Chelsea

65–9 Lots Road, London SW10

020 7393 3900

Bonhams, Knightsbridge

Montpelier Street

Knightsbridge

London SW7 1HH

020 7393 3900

Christie's, South Kensington

85 Old Brompton Road

London SW7 3LD

020 7581 7611

Phillips

101 New Bond Street

London W1Y 0AS

020 7629 6602

Sotheby's

34–35 New Bond St

London W1A 2AA

020 7293 5283

Publisher's note:

Telephone codes for London are changing from April 22nd 2000. 0181 will become 020 8+telephone number and 0171 will become 020 7+telephone number. After April 22nd 2000 you will be able to dial without using the 020 code if you are within the same code area. Until April 22nd 2000 you must dial the full telephone number including the 020 code regardless.

bibliography

Ball, Joan Dubbs, *Costume Jewelers: The Golden Age of Design,* Schiffer, 1990

Bennett Levy, Michael, *TV is King,* MBL Publications, 1994

Bishop, Christina, *Miller's Collecting Kitchenware,* Miller's, Octopus Publishing Group Ltd, 1995

Black, J. Anderson and Garland, Madge, *A History of Fashion,* Orbis Publishing 1975

Chenoune, Farid, *A History of Men's Fashion,* Flammarion, 1993

Corson, Richard, *Fashions in Makeup,* Peter Owen, 1972

Dooner, Kate E., *Plastic Handbags, Sculpture to Wear,* Schiffer, 1993

Ferragamo, Salvatore, *The Art of the Shoe,* Centro Di, 1987

Fiell, Charlotte & Peter, *Modern Chairs,* Taschen, 1993

Gabor, Mark, *The Pin-Up, A Modest History,* Andre Deutsch, 1972

Garner, Philippe, *Twentieth Century Furniture,* Phaidon, 1980

Gibbings, Sarah, *The Tie,* Studio Editions, 1990

Gordon, Angie, *Twentieth Century Costume Jewellery,* Adasia International 1990

Heiremans, Mark, *Art Glass from Murano,* 1993

Hiesinger, K.B. and Marcus, G.H., *Landmarks of Twentieth Century Design,* Abbeville Press, 1993

Hillier, Bevis, *The Style of the Century, 1900–1980,* The Herbert Press, 1986

Howell, Georgina, *In Vogue, Six Decades of Fashion,* Allen Lane, 1975

Katz, Sylvia, *Classic Plastics,* Thames and Hudson, 1984

Larkin, Colin (ed), *The Guinness Encyclopaedia of Popular Music,* Guinness Publishing, 1993

MacCarthy, Fiona, *British Design Since 1880,* Lund Humphries, 1982

McDowell, Colin, *Hats,* Thames and Hudson, 1992

Marly, Diana de, *Christian Dior,* B.T. Batsford, 1990

Martin, Richard (ed), *Contemporary Fashion,* St James Press, 1996

Massey, Anne, *Interior Design of the 20th Century,* Thames and Hudson, 1991

Mauries, Patrick, *Fornasetti, Designer of Dreams,* Thames and Hudson, 1991

Metasti, Rosa Barovier, *Venetian Glass 1890–1990,* Arsenale Editrice, 1992

Naylor, Colin (ed), *Contemporary Designers,* St James Press, 1990

Niblett, Kathy, *Dyamic Design, The British Pottery Industry 1940–1980,* Stoke-on-Trent Museum and Art Gallery, 1990

Opie, Jennifer, *Scandinavian Ceramics and Glass in the Twentieth Century,* Victoria and Albert Museum, 1989

Peat, Alan, *Midwinter: A Collectors' Guide,* Cameron & Hollis, 1992

Philadelphia Museum of Art, *Design Since 1945,* Exhibition Catalogue, 1983

Polak, Ada, *Modern Glass,* Faber and Faber, 1962

Polhemus, Ted, *Street Style,* Thames and Hudson, 1995

Potter, Margaret & Alexander, *Interiors,* John Murrary, 1957

Porter, Catherine, *Miller's Collecting Books,* Miller's, Octopus Publishing Group Ltd, 1995

Probert, Christina, *Swimwear in Vogue,* Thames and Hudson, 1981

Schoeser, Mary, *Fabrics and Wallpapers, Twentieth Century Design,* Bell & Hyman, 1986

Schoeser, Mary and Rufey Celia, *English and American Textiles,* Thames and Hudson, 1989

Seymour-Smith, Martin, *Novels and Novelists,* St. Martins's Press, 1980

Smith, Nigel, *Britain since 1945,* Wayland Publishers, 1990

Sommer, Robert Langley, *Toys of our Generation,* Magana Books, 1992

Sparke, Penny, *Furniture, Twentieth Century Design,* Bell & Hyman, 1986

Sparke, Penny, *Electrical Appliances, Twentieth Century Design,* Bell & Hyman, 1987

Stoneback, Bruce and Diane, *Matchbox Toys,* The Apple Press, 1993

Tibballs, Geoff, *The Guinness Book of Innovations,* Guinness Publishing, 1994

Trasko, Mary, *Heavenly Soles,* Abbeville, 1989

index

Page numbers in *italic*
refer to illustrations,
those in **bold** refer to
main entries

Aarnio, Eero 22, 24
Ackery, London 95
"Acrilica" lamp 41
"Action Man" 112, *115*
Adelto 24
afghan coat *89*
Airbournet 28
Alfie 132
"Alogena" lamp 41
Alternative London 135
"Alveston" range *67*
American furniture **30–1,**
   34, 36, 39
Anderson, Gerry 116
Andrea 99
Anello & Davide 105
Antonioni, Michelangelo
   111, 128, 129
"Apollo Lunar Module"
   toy *113*
Archizoom 21
"Arco" lamp *41*
"Ariel" glass *62*
Ark 72
ARPE 51
Art Deco 35, 39
Art Nouveau 31, 35, 75, 84
Arthur Wood & Sons 58
Artifort 29, 35
Artwoods 120
Ashley, Laura 87
ashtrays *61*
Asko 24
"Assimetrico" range *65*
Aurea 45
autographs 118
Avedon, Richard 74

Avengers 92, 116, 133
Ayres & Co., L. S. 106

BA "1171" chair 33
Babb, Paul 78
"Babe Rainbow" picture *73*
babydoll nightie *91*
badges 100, *101*
Bailey, David 72, 105
Baker, Carroll 91
Balenciaga 80
"Ball" chair *24*
Ballito 91
Banks, Lynne Reid 132
Barbarella 131
"Barbie" doll 112, *114*
"Barboy" unit *37*
Bardot, Brigitte 31, 80,
   86, *123,* 131
Barker Bros 57
Bartlett, David 26
Bates, John 82
Batman car 112, *117*
Batzner, Helmut 22, 25, 33
Baxter, Geoffrey 64
Bazaar 100, 133
"Bazaar" dress *78*
Beach Boys *125*
bean bags *16*
Beatles
   design influence 71
   fashion influence 77, 91,
      104, 105, 108, 131
   hairstyles *99*
   memorabilia *118, 119, 121*
   posters *74*
   records *118*
bell bottoms *85,* 107
Belle de Jour 128
Bellini, Mario 46
belts *81, 95,* 100
Bender, Lee 78
Bernini 20, 36

Bertoia, Harry 30
Best, George 107, 109
"Best Tea" tins *53*
"Biarritz" sandals *94*
Biba 15, 35, 78, 79, 86, 93,
   100, 101
"Biba" table *35*
Bieffeplast 38
"Big O" 74
Birkin, Jane 123, 129
Birtwell, Celia 79
Black, Cilla 123
Blackman, Honor 92,
   116, 133
Blake, Peter 73, 119
"Blast-Off!" game *113*
blouses *84, 85*
"Blow" chair 16, *17*
Blow-Up 27, 128, *129*
Blue Peter annual *130*
"Boby" trolley *38*
body stocking 81, 83, 90
Boffi 37
Bofinger, Wilhelm 33
"Bofinger" chair *25*
Bohan, Mark 80
Bolan, Marc 123
Bonetto, Rodolfo 33
Bonham, John 127
Boogie Nights 45
books *122, 129, 130,* **132–3**
boots *92–3,* 105
Boro 29
Boutique 134
"boutique crepe" *86*
Bowie, David 122
bowls *54, 56, 60, 61*
Bracegirdle, Arthur 44
Brauer, Otto 62
Braun 44, 46, 49
Breakfast at Tiffany's 128
Brent, Sidney 106
Bridgen, Allison 54

Britain
   fashion design **78–9,** *82,*
      85–7, 88, 104, 106, 108, 109
   furniture **26–7,** *35*
   glass *60,* **64–5**
   lighting *42, 43*
   metalware *66, 67*
   British Home Stores 42
brocade *86,* 107
Brown, Barbara 57, 68
"Bubble" glass *65*
Buñuel, Luis 128
Burgess, Anthony 133
Burke, John 129
Burroughs, William S. 132
Bustop 78

Cadbury/Typhoo 53
Cadec, Mme 51
Calderon 96
Cale, John 102
camisole *86*
Captain Scarlett 116
"Can" coffee pot *56*
caps *97, 98*
"Caravel" cutlery *66*
Cardin, Pierre 80, 81, 104,
   106
Carlton Ware 58
Carnaby Street 15, 77, 78, 82,
   104, 107, 108, 109
cars, toy *116, 117, 125*
cartoons *130*
Casa Pupo 70
casserole dishes *51*
Castelli 19
Castiglioni brothers 20, 41
Castlecliff, USA 102
Catch-22 132, 133
Cathy Come Home 128, *129*
CEI 39
ceramics **54–9**
Chad Valley 112

chainmail 80, *81, 95*
chairs **16–31**
chaises longues *23, 28*
Chanel, Coco 80
Chaumette, Paris 58
"Chemist Print" range *58*
Christie, Julie 129
"Cifra 3" clock *49*
Clappison, John 56
Clapton, Eric 74, 120, 126
Clark, Ossie 78, 79
Clark, Paul 49, 52, 58
Clendinning, Max 27
clocks *49*
Clockwork Orange 133
clothes **76–109,** *127*
coasters *53*
coats *84, 89*
coffee pots *55, 56, 57, 58, 66*
Colani, Luigi 22
Colombo, Joe 16, 18–19, 36, 37, 38, 39, 41, 65
"Combi Centre" unit *36*
Comfort 18
"Comfortable Corsets" coffee service *58*
"Compact" tableware *51*
"Cone" chair *23*
Connery, Sean 128, 129
Cooper, Susie 56
Corgi toys *116, 117*
cosmetics 90, 96, **98–9**
"Cosmic '60s" 135
counter-culture 97, 111, 132, 134, 135
Courrèges, André 80, 81, 92, 93, 94, 96, 97
"Couture Future" jacket *81*
Cream 74, 127
Crestworth 42
"Cricket" telephone *48*
Crown Devon 52, 56
cruets *58, 59*
culottes *80*
Curtain, Hoyt 130
curtains 68, *70*
cushions *31, 71*

cutlery *66*
"Cylinda-Line" range *66*

Dad's Army 128
Dale, Dick *125*
Daleks *117*
Daltry, Roger 89, 121
"Dalu" lamp *40*
Dam Things 114
Danese 41
Daniels, Norman 133
Dansk International Designs 50
David, Elizabeth 51
David Anderson 102
David Whitehead 69
Day, Robin 26
de Santillana, Ludovico 60
Dean's Rag Book 112
decanters *60*
"Delphis" collection *54*
Delton NY 107
Deneuve, Catherine 128
Design Centre 68
Design M. Munich 39
"DF 2000" furniture *39*
Dinky toys *116*
Dior 80
"Djinn" seating *28*
Dodo Designs 53, 66, 67, 73
dolls *112, 114, 115, 118*
doll's houses *112*
Donovan 104, 124
Doomsday Affair 133
Dors, Diana 114
Doubinski FrPres 39
Dr Who 112, *117*
drawstring top *88*
dresses **78–83, 85–7**
drugs 34, 42, 77, 88, 97, 107, 111, 132, 135
"Drunken Bricklayer" vase *64*
"Dune" dress *82*
Dunn, Nell 128, 129
Dupont, Patrice 45
Dylan, Bob *74,* 104, 124, 131, 135

Eames, Charles & Ray 30, 34, 35
Early Learning Centre 112
Easy Rider 75
"Eclisse" lamp *40*
Edwardia 109
Ekberg, Anita 128
"Elda" chair *18*
Emergency Ward 10 130
English, Mike 135
Erik Jorgensen 22
Exton, Raymond 101

Faithfull, Marianne 123
"Falkland" lamp *41*
false eyelashes *99*
fans *49*
fashion
British **78–9,** *82, 85–7, 88, 104, 106, 108, 109*
French *80–1, 82, 85, 92, 93, 95*
men's **104–9**
women's **76–103**
Fellini, Frederico 128
Ferrieri, Anna Castelli 38
"Fiesta" plate *57*
films **128–9**
"Fine" pottery *57*
flatware *66*
Fleming, Ian 129
Flexiform-Prima 18
Flintstones record *130*
Flos 41, 43
flower power 35, 88, 98, 104
Foale & Tuffin 88, 101, 115
"Focus" pattern *57*
Fonda, Jane 128, 131
Four Tops 124
France
audio equipment *45*
fashion design **80–1,** *82, 85, 92, 93, 95*
furniture **28–9,** *35*
lighting *42*
Franck, Kaj 63
Frisbee 112

Fritz Hansen 23
furniture
American **30–1,** *34, 36, 39*
British **26–7,** *35*
German *22, 25, 33, 39*
Italian **16–21,** *33, 36–7, 38–9*
Scandinavian **22–4,** *37*
storage **36–9**
see also under individual items

Gainsbourg, Serge 123
Galt 112
Gandalf's Garden 134
"Garden Egg" chair *25*
Gatti, Piero 16
Gavina 16, 20
"Gaytime" design *59*
Germany
ceramics *55*
furniture *22, 25, 33, 39*
technological design *46, 49*
Gernreich, Rudi 82, 90, 91, 96
Ghyczy, Peter 22, 25
"GI Joe" 112, *115*
"Ginger Group" dress *85*
Givenchy, Hubert de 80
glass **60–5**
Glasshouse 60
"Glitter" lamp *42*
Goddard, Jean-Luc 111
Gold brothers 108
gollywog *112*
"Granny Takes a Trip" 53
graphic design 71, 72, 75
Gray's Pottery 58
"Grillo" telephone *48*
Grundig 44
Gufram 17
"Gulvase" range *62*

Haase, John 129
Habitat 15, 19, 26, 30, 36, 43, 50, 51, 52
Hagler, Stanley 102
Hair 79, 98
hairstyles 77, 98, *99,* 104

Hallmark 83
handbags 92, 95, *100*
hangers *38, 78, 104*
hanging chair *25*
Hanna & Barbera 130
Hansel, Merrick 69
Hansen, Hans 102
Harris, Michael 64
Hasbro 115
hats 92, *97, 104*
Heals 68
Heller, Joseph 132, 133
Heller Designs 51
Hemmings, David 129, 131
Hendrix, Jimi *74,* 126
Hepburn, Audrey 80, 128
Herman Miller 23, 30, 34
"Hi Brow" boots *93*
hi-fi systems *45, 46*
hippies
    fashions *75,* **88–9,** *104, 107*
    hairstyles 98
    homestyle *31,* 40, *42, 70*
    jewellery 100
Holdaway, Bernard 27
Holmegaard Glassworks 62
Homepride flour-graders 53
"Hoodwinks" *99*
Hornsea Pottery 56
House and Garden 135
Hulanicki, Barbara *see* Biba
Hull Traders Ltd 27
Hullabaloo 93
Hung on You 86
Hunt, Martin 56

I-glass range *63*
I Was Lord Kitchener's Valet
    52, 53, 58, 108
ice-bucket *50*
Illsley, Lesley 54
inflatable chairs *17, 31*
International Times 134
Italian Job 24
Italtel 48
Italy
    films 128, 129

furniture **16–21,** *33, 36,*
    37, 38–9
glass **60–1,** *65*
lighting *40, 40–1, 43*
technological design *46,*
    48, 49
Ittala Glassworks 63

Jackets *81,* 89, *104, 105, 106,*
    107, 109
Jacobsen, Arne 23, 66
Jagger, Mick 79, 105
Jalk, Grete 22
James Bond merchandise
    112, *129*
jeans *88, 89*
Jefferson, Robert 54
Jefferson Airplane 127
Jensen, Georg 66, 102
Jetsons record *130*
jewellery **100–3,** *119*
Johannes Hansen 22
Johns, Jasper 58
John's Children 123
Johnson & Johnson 108
Johnson Brothers 57
JRM Designs 52
Jules et Jim 97
JVC 44

Kaftans *88, 89*
Kartell 19, 33, 38, 39
Kennedy, Jackie 80, 97,
    102, 114
"Keracolour" television 44
Kesey, Ken 97
Kinetic Art *102*
King, Perry A. 48
King's Road 77, 82, 109
Kinks 106, 122
Kirkhams 58
kitchen ware **50–3,** *58, 59*
Kleptomania 109
Knoll, Florence 34, 35, 36
Knoll International 16, 30, 36
Koppel, Henning 66
Kosta Glassworks 63

Kubrick, Stanley 133

L-*Shaped Room 132*
La Dolce Vita 128
Laker, Sir Freddie 53
lamps **40–3,** *54*
lampshades *43*
Lane, Kenneth J. 103
"Lassi" range *62*
"Lava" lamp 40, *42*
Le Carré, John 132
Le Creuset *51*
Led Zeppelin 127
lemonade set *59*
Lennon, John *74,* 97, 104
Leonard 99
Lester, Richard 129
Levis *89*
Liberty 88
lighting **40–3,** *54*
Lindstrand, Vicke 63
lingerie 81, 83, **90–1**
"Liza Peta" dress *82*
Loewy, Raymond 39
Loftus, Richard 102
loons 85, *107*
Lord John 108
Lord Nelson Pottery 59
Lord of the Rings 134
luggage *97*
Lulu 123
Lundin, Ingeborg 62
Lutken, Per 62

Magazines 71, 72, **134–5**
Magic Roundabout
    merchandise *43, 52*
Magistretti, Vico 19, 40
Magnetic Man 133
make up *see* cosmetics
"Malitte" seating *16–17*
Man from U.N.C.L.E. 117, 133
Mao Tse Tung *49*
Marks & Spencer 83
Marley, Bob 124
Marx 117
Mastroianni, Marcello 128

"Mates" jacket *107*
Matta, Roberto 16
Mattel 114
Maurer-Becher, Dorothea 39
Max, Peter 31, 135
maxi length *87*
"Maxima" seating *27*
McCallum, David *117*
McCartney, Paul *118*
McCulloch, Peter 68
McDowell, Malcolm 133
McGowan, Cathy 98
McNee, Patrick *116,* 133
Mdina Glass 64
Mellor, David 66, 67
metalware **66–7**
Mettoy 113
Midwinter 57
"Mies" chair *21*
military influences *69,* 104,
    106, 108
Millie 124
mini length *79, 80, 81, 82,*
    83, 87
"Minikitchen" *37*
Miss Selfridge 81
Modernism 27, 34, 35,
    36, 133
mods 80, 104, 105
Molinary, Rossi 20
Mondrian 80, 82, 84
money boxes *55, 58*
Monkees 121, *125*
Moon, Keith 121
"moon girl" collection 81, 92
"Moon light *40*
Morphy Richards 50
Morris, Tony 54
Moulton bikes 112
Mourgue, Olivier 28
"Mouse" lamp *41*
Move 122
Mr Fish 106
Mr Freedom 109
"Mr Smith" golly *112*
Mr Tambourine Man 74
mugs *52, 58*

Munari, Bruno 41
Murano Glassworks 61
Murdoch, Peter 26

Naked Lunch 132
Naughton, Bill 132
"Nehru" jacket 109
"Newton's Cradle" 67
Nichols, Mike 133
Nicola 31
nightdress 91
Nova 39, 134
novelties 46, 49, 58, 61, 67
Nuutajarvi Glassworks 63

Old England 102
Old Hall Tableware 67
Oldenburg, Claes 31
Olivetti 48
Op Art
  book design 135
  in design 30, 35, 45, 52, 56
  in fashion 82, 91, 95, 96, 101
  textiles 69
Orrefors Glassworks 62
"Ox" chair 22
Oz 74, 135

Package holidays,
  influence of 53
Palitoy 114, 115, 117
Pallenberg, Anita 131
Pan 129
Panton, Verner 22, 23, 37,
  40, 69
"Panton" chair 23
pantyhose see tights
Paolini, Cesare 16
Paolozzi, Eduardo 75
Paper Airplane Book 135
paper dress 83
paper furniture 26, 27, 34, 37
paper jewellery 100
paper lampshades 43
Party of Sussex 92
"Pastille" chair 24
patches 101

patchwork 88
"Paul" doll 115
Paulin, Pierre 28, 29, 35
"Peacock" chair 30, 31
Pedigree 115
Pelham 121
Pennebaker, D.A. 131
Perspective Designs Ltd 49
Pesce, Gaetano 17
Petulia 129
Philips 45
Pianon, Alessandro 61
pictures 72–3
pin-ups 72, 73
Pink Floyd 126
Piretti, Giancarlo 19
plates 57, 58, 59
Platner, Warren 30
"Play-plax" Squares 113
"Plia" chair 19
Plunkett, William 27
Plus-Linje 23
polo shirt 105
Poltronova 21
"Polyprop" chair 26
poncho 89
Poole Pottery 54
Pop Art 31, 58, 71, 72, 82,
  95, 108
pop memorabilia 118–27, 131
pop music, influence of 68,
  74–5, 118–19, 121–2, 125,
  127, 131
"Pop" record player 46
"Pop Singers" puppets 121
Porter, Thea 79
Portmeirion 55, 56, 58
posters 73–5, 128, 129, 130,
  131
Poul Jeppeson 22
Prisoner 24
Private Eye 52
Proctor, Pam 78
protest movement, influence
  of 49, 71, 101
psychedelic patterns 28, 29,
  31, 52, 59, 91, 97, 135

Pucci, Emilio 84, 91, 96
PVC 17, 84, 93, 95, 100
Pyrex 51

Quant, Mary
  autobiography 133
  daisy logo 52, 93, 98, 100
  fashion designs 85, 90, 92,
    93, 96, 98, 99, 100
  influence of 78, 82, 83, 91
  kitchenware 50
Queen 134
Queensberry, David 54, 55
Quistgaard, Jens H. 50
Quorum 78, 79

Rabanne, Paco 80, 81, 95, 96
Race Furniture 27
Radio 1 annual 122
Radio Luxembourg book 122
radios 44, 46–7
raincoat 84
Rainey, Mike 86
Rams, Dieter 22, 25, 46, 49
Ramshaw, Wendy 100
Ravenhead Glass 65
Ready Steady Go 98
record players 45, 46
records 31, 116, 118, 119–27,
  129, 130
Redgrave, Vanessa 128
Reeves, Martha 124
Regiani 41
Renoir/Matisse 95
Reuter Produkts 25
Rhodes, Zandra 69
"Ribbon" chair 29
Richard, Cliff 116
Rigg, Diana 116, 133
Riihimaki Glassworks 62
Riley, Bridget 56, 101
Roberts, Tommy 104, 109
Roberts radio 47
Robor Ltd 112
rock music see pop
Roffey, Maureen 112
Rolling Stones 75, 107, 120

Ross, Diana 124
Royal Copenhagen 55
Royal Tudor Ware 57
rugs 70
Rylands, Patrick 113

Saarinen, Eero 30, 34, 35
"Safari" seating 21
Saint toys 117
"Salome" placemats 52
"San Luca" chair 20
sandals 94
Sanderson wallpaper 14
Sandford, Jeremy 129
Sapper, Richard 48
Sarpaneva, Timo 63
Sassoon, Vidal 99
saucepans 51
Saunders Enterprises 104
Scandinavia
  furniture 22–4, 37
  glass 60, 62–3
  jewellery 102
  kitchenware 50
  lighting 40
  metalware 66
  textiles 69
Scarpa, Tobia 43
Schofield, Jean 27
Scolari, D'Urbinio, Lomazzi
  & De Pas 17
Scott Lester Organisation 109
seating 16–31
Seguso Vetri d'Arte 61
"Selene" chair 19
Sellers, Irvine 107
settees 20–1, 31
Shapiro, Helen 123
Sharp, Martin 74, 135
Shaw, Sandy 94
Sheridan, Tony 119
shirts 71, 89, 105, 107, 108
shoes 92–5, 96, 105
shorts 85
shoulder bags 83, 92, 95, 96
Shrimpton, Jean 72, 77, 78,
  87, 99

"Sienna" pattern 57
"Sindy" doll 112, *115*
Singleton, Valerie *130*
Sirota, Benny 54
skateboards 112
skirts *81, 83, 88*
Small Faces 120
"Smart Miss" suit *83*
"Smash" Martians *53*
Smashing Bird 129
"Smoke" range 65
social realism 111, 128, 129, 132
"Soft Pad" chair *30*
Solari & Co. 49
Sottsass, Ettore 48
space, influence of 40, 44–5, 113, 122
space-age look 20, 39, 42, 80, 81, 92
"Space ball" radio-cassette *45*
"Space Hopper" 112, *113*
spice jars *53*
"Sputnik" television *44*
Spy Who Came in from the Cold 132
St Laurent, Yves 82
Standard Radio Corporation 47
Starr, Ringo *104*
Stelton, A.S. 66
Stephen, John 104, 106, 108
Steptoe and Son 128
stockings 90, *91*
Stoppino, Giotto 33, 39
storage
    containers 52, 53
    furniture 36–9
Strawberry Alarm Clock *31*
string pictures *72*
"Studiocraft" planter *56*
sunglasses 100, *101*
"Super Colour" television *44*
"Superonda" settee *20*
Supremes 124
surf music 125

swimwear *91*
Swinging London 66, 78, 82, 108, 111
Sydenham, Guy 54

T. Rex 123
"Tab" chair *26*
table mats *52*
tables **32–5**
tableware *51, 52, 53,* 56–9, 66–7
Tait, Jessie 57
Take Six 106
Tamla Motown 124
tea caddies *53*
tea set *67*
"Technicus" fabric *69*
technology **44–9**
Telefunken 47
telephones *48*
television, influence of 43, 52, 53, 71, 112, 116–17, 125, 133
television programmes 112, 116–17, 125, 128, 130–1, 133
televisions *44*
Tender Tootsies, Canada *92*
Teodoro, Franco 16
textiles **68–71**
Thomas, Germany 59
Thompson, Jan 54
Thunderbirds toys *116,* 121
ties *106*
tights 90, *91, 92*
"Tiny Tears" *114*
toaster *50*
Tolkein, J.R.R. 134
Tommy Nutter 86
Tomorrow's World 128, 130
"Tomotom" furniture *27, 35*
Top of the Pops 128, 130
"Topo" lamp *41*
"Total Furnishing Unit" 39
"total" look 90, *96*
"Totem" coffee pot *55*
"Tourneraj" chair *17*

Townsend, Pete 108, 121, 126
"Toy" chair *20*
toys **112–17**, *125, 132*
Trace, Chris *130*
transistor radios 44, *47*
tray *67*
Trendon 113
"Tressie" doll 112
Trifari 103
Trimfit USA 91
Troika 54, 73
trolls *114*
trousers *85, 107, 108, 127*
Truffaut, François 97
"Tube" chair *18*
"Tulip" furniture 35
tumblers *59, 65*
Turnbull & Asser 106
Turner, Philip 56
Twiggy *76,* 77, 78, 91, 95, 98, 99
2001: A Space Odyssey 28, 45

Underground scene 97, 111, 132, 134, 135
underwear *67, 81, 83,* **90–1**
Union Jack in design 58, 66, *67, 108*
"Universale" chair *19*
"UP" furniture *16–17*
Up the Junction 128, *129*

Vadim, Roger *131*
"Valentine" typewriter 44, *48*
Valle, Gino 49
Van Buren, Abigail 94
"Varsity Shop" jacket *106*
Vasarely, Victor 56, 101
vases *54, 55, 60, 61, 62, 63, 64, 65*
Vaughn, Robert *117*
Velvet Underground 102
Venini Glassworks 60, 61
"Videosphere" television *44*
Vignella, Massimo & Lella 51
"Vision 2000" 45

Vistosi Glassworks 61
Vitra 23, 30

Waistcoats *84, 86*
Walker, Edward Craven 42
"Wall-All" unit *39*
Warhol, Andy 68, 71, 105, 108
Washington Pottery 59
watches *98, 102*
Way In 100
Weckstrom, Bjorn 102
Wedgwood 65
Wegner, Hans 22
Weiss, Rhienhold 49
Welch, Robert 66, 67
"Weltron" hifi *45*
Wesselmann, Tom 31
West Coast influence 73, 85, 88, 125, 132
"wet" look *93*
Weymouth, Nigel 135
Whitefriars 60, 64
Who 89, 108, 121
Wiggin, J. & J. 67
wigs 97, 98, *99*
Williams-Ellis, Susan 55, 58
Williamson, Alexander Hardie 65
Woodstock 89, 127
Woolworth's 99
Wright, John 27

Yard Birds 120
Yellow Submarine toy *132*
Yogi Bear record *130*

Z-Cars annual 130
Zanota 17
Zanuso, Marco 48

acknowledgments

key

b   bottom
c   centre
t   top
l   left
r   right

AA   Advertising Archives
A   Alfie's
BC   Beatcity
B   Boom!
BON   Bonhams
BAL   Bridgeman Art Library
CC   Chelsea Clocks
CHI   Childhood Memories
CI   Christie's Images
CSK   Christie's, South Kensington
DV   Delta of Venus
FF   Freeforms
GIN   Ginnell Gallery
HUL   Hulton Getty Picture Collection
MEM   Memory Lane
MILL   Miller's Publications
MOD   Modern Age Vintage Clothing
NL   Nikki Lynes
NIG   Nigel Williams Rare Books
OPG   Octopus Publishing Group Ltd
PB   Planet Bazaar
RAD   Radio Days
ROK   Rokit Ltd
S&T   Steinberg & Tolkien
SH   Stella Harding, Camden
TAR   Target Gallery
20:21   Twenty Twenty One
Z   Zambesi

photographers

IB   Ian Booth
TR   Tim Ridley
AJ   Andy Johnson

Front jacket t OPG/TR/Z; **Front jacket**, c OPG/TR/NL; **Front jacket**, bl OPG/TR/S&T; **Front jacket flap** OPG/TR/A; **Back jacket**, t OPG/TR/20:21; **Back jacket**, c OPGTR/DV; **Back jacket**, b OPG/TR/B; **Back jacket flap** OPG/TR/NL; 1 OPG/TR/TAR; 2 OPG/TR/Z; 3 OPG/TR/20:21; 4-5 OPG/TR/20:21; 8-9 HUL; 10 l OPG/TR/PB; 10 r OPG/TR/A; 11 l MILL/Frasers; 11 r MILL/RD; 11 c MILL; 12 l OPG/TR/TAR; 12 r OPG/TR/A; 13 l OPG/TR/A; 13 r OPG/TR/A; 13 c OPG/TR/A; 14 AA; 16 t OPG/TR/PB; 16-17 b CI/Roberto Sebastian Matta; 17 t OPG/TR/20:21; 17 cl MILL/IB; 17 cr OPG/TR/20:21; 17 b OPG/Giorgio Ceretti; Piero Derossi; Ricardo Rossi; 18 t BAL/Private Collection; 18 b CI/Joe Colombo; 19 t OPG/TR/20:21; 19 c OPG/TR/Z; 19 b OPG/TR/PB; 20 CI; 21 CI; 22 t CI; 22 b OPG/TR/20:21; 23 tl OPG/TR/20:21; 23 tr OPG/TR/PB; 23 bl MILL/CSK; 23 br OPG/TR/20:21; 24 t MILL; 24 b 20:21; 25 tl OPG/TR/PB; 25 tr OPG/TR/PB; 25 bl OPG/TR/20:21; 25 br MILL; 26 t Robin Day/Hille International; 26 b OPG/TR/TAR; 27 tl OPG/TR/TAR; 27 tr OPG/TR/TAR; 27 bl OPG/TR/20:21; 27 br OPG/TR/20:21; 28 t OPG/IB/BON; 28 b OPG/TR; 29 t OPG/TR/20:21; 29 c OPG/TR/20:21; 29 b OPG/TR/20:21; 30 t OPG/TR/20:21; 30 b OPG/TR/20:21; 31 t OPG/TR/PB; 31 cl OPG/TR/DV; 31 cr OPG/TR/DV; 31 br MILL; 32 t OPG/TR/B; 32 b OPG/TR/B; 33 t OPG/TR/PB; 33 c OPG/TR/PB; 33 b OPG/TR/Z; 34 t OPG/TR/20:21; 34 b OPG/TR/A; 35 t OPG/TR/B; 35 c MILL; 35 b OPG/TR/TAR; 36 t OPG/TR/20:21; 36 b MILL; 37 tl MILL; 37 tc MILL/CSK; 37 tr OPG/TR/TAR; 37 b CI; 38 tl OPG/TR/Z; 38 tc OPG/TR/PB; 38 tr OPG/TR/B; 38 b OPG/TR/20:21; 39 t OPG/TR/PB; 39 c OPG/TR/PB; 39 b OPG/TR/20:21; 40 tl OPG/TR/PB; 40 tr OPG/TR/20:21; 40 br OPG/TR/PB; 41 r OPG/TR/20:21; 41 tl OPG/TR/20:21; 41 bl OPG/TR/B; 42 l OPG/TR/B; 42 tr OPG/TR/B; 42 c OPG/TR/B; 42 br OPG/TR/Z; 43 tl OPG/TR/Z; 43 tr OPG/TR/NL; 43 c OPG/TR/PB; 43 b OPG/TR/PB; 44 t OPGAJ/BON; 44 b OPG/TR/B; 45 t OPG/TR/B; 45 c OPG/TR/B; 45 b OPG/TR/B; 46 t OPG/TR/20:21; 46 b OPG/TR/TAR; 47 tl OPG/TR/A; 47 tr OPG/TR/Z; 47 c OPG/TR/TAR; 47 b OPG/TR/A; 48 tl MILL/GINN; 48 tc OPG/TR/20:21; 48 tr OPG/TR/20:21; 48 b OPG/AJ/BON; 49 t OPG/TR/Z; 49 cl OPG/TR/TAR; 49 cr MILL/CC; 49 b OPG/TR/20:21; 50 t MILL; 50 b OPG/TR/NL; 51 t OPG/AJ/BON; 51 c t OPG/TR/Z; 51 c b OPG/TR/Author's collection; 51 b OPG/TR/NL; 52 t OPG/TR/TAR; 52 cl OPG/TR/TAR; 52 c OPG/TR/Z; 52 b OPG/TR/Z; 53 cl OPG/TR/Z; 53 cr MILL/GIN; 53 b MILL/David Huxtable; 54 t MILL; 54 bl OPG/BON; 54 br MILL; 55 t OPG/TR/Z; 55 c OPG/TR/Z; 55 b Portmeirion Potteries Ltd.; 56 t MILL; 56 c OPG/TR/Home Service; 56 b MILL; 57 t OPG/TR/Z; 57 c OPG/TR/TAR; 57 cl OPG/SH; 57 b MILL; 58 t OPG/TR/TAR; 58 b OPG/TR/TAR; 58 c b OPG/TR/PB; 58 bl OPG/TR/PB; 58 br OPG/TR/PB; 59 t OPG/TR/Z; 59 c OPG/TR/Z; 59 b OPG/TR/Z; 60 t OPG/TR/FF; 60 b OPG/TR/Z; 61 t OPG/TR/B; 61 c OPG/TR/B; 61 b OPG/AJ; 62 t OPG/TR/Glassforms/FF; 62 c OPG/TR/PB; 62 b OPG/TR/B; 63 tl OPG/TR/B; 63 tr OPG/TR/TAR; 63 b OPG/TR/Glassforms; 64 t OPG/TR/PB; 64 c OPG/TR/PB; 64 b OPG/TR/B; 65 t OPG/TR/B; 65 cr OPG/TR/PB; 65 cl OPG/TR/TAR; 65 b MILL/CSK; 66 t OPG/TR/20:21; 66 b OPG/AJ/Fay Lucas; 67 t OPG/TR/TAR; 67 cl OPG/TR/TAR; 67 cr MILL/GIN; 67 b OPG/TR/TAR; 68 t OPG/TR/20:21; 68 c MILL; 68 b OPG/TR/20:21; 69 t OPG/TR/20:21; 69 c OPG/TR/20:21; 69 cl OPG/TR/20:21; 69 bl OPG/TR/20:21; 69 br OPG/TR/20:21; 70 t OPG/TR/Author's collection; 70 c OPG/TR/B; 70 b OPG/TR/Z; 71 tl OPG/TR/TAR; 71 tr MILL/BC; 71 c OPG/TR/NL; 71 bl OPG/TR/TAR; 72 t OPG/TR/TAR; 72 b OPG/TR/Z; 73 t OPG/TR/B; 73 tl OPG/TR/A; 73 bc OPG/TR/TAR; 73 br OPG/TR/TAR; 74 tl MILL/Russell, Baldwin & Bright; 74 tr OPG/TR/TAR; 74 b OPG/TR/TAR; 75 tl OPG/TR/TAR; 75 tr OPG/TR/TAR; 75 c OPG/TR/TAR; 75 b OPG/TR/TAR; 76 HUL; 78 t OPG/TR/NL; 78 bl OPG/TR/DV; 78 br OPG/TR/NL; 79 tr OPG/TR/NL; 79 tl OPG/TR/NL; 79 c OPG/TR/S&T; 79 b OPG/TR/S&T; 80 t OPG/TR/S&T; 80 b OPG/TR/S&T; 81 tr OPG/TR/NL; 81 cl OPG/IB/CSK; 81 cr OPG/TR/A/Persiflage; 81 b OPG/TR/20:21; 82 tl OPG/TR/NL; 82 tr OPG/TR/MOD; 82 b OPG/TR/S&T; 83 tl OPG/TR/RAD; 83 tr OPG/TR/20:21; 83 c OPG/TR/NL; 83 b OPG/TR/S&T; 84 t OPG/TR/MOD; 84 c OPG/TR/RAD; 84 b OPG/TR/DV; 85 tl OPG/TR/A; 85 tr OPG/TR/A; 85 bl OPG/TR/S&T; 85 br OPG/TR/S&T; 86 t OPG/TR/NL; 86 tr OPG/TR/RAD; 86 c OPG/TR/RAD; 86 b OPG/TR/NL; 87 l OPG/TR/NL; 87 r OPG/TR/S&T; 87 c OPG/TR/A; 88 tl OPG/TR/A; 88 tr OPG/TR/A; 88 b OPG/TR/A; 89 tl OPG/TR/NL; 89 tr OPG/TR/NL; 89 cr MILL/ROK; 89 c tl OPG/TR/NL; 89 c bl OPG/TR/NL; 89 br OPG/TR/ROK; 90 r OPG/TR/PB; 90 tl OPG/TR/A/Sparkle Moore; 90 t OPG/TR/A; 91 tl OPG/TR/RAD; 91 tr OPG/TR/A/Sparkle Moore; 91 cl OPG/TR/A/Persiflage; 91 c OPG/TR/A; 91 b OPG/TR/A; 92 t OPG/TR/A; 92 tr OPG/TR/A; 92 br OPG/TR/NL; 93 t OPG/TR/NL; 93 c OPG/TR/B; 93 b OPG/TR/MOD; 94 t OPG/TR/RAD; 94 cl OPG/TR/NL; 94 cr OPG/TR/RAD; 94 bl OPG/TR/NL; 94 br OPG/TR/NL; 95 tl OPG/TR/A/Christobal; 95 tr OPG/TR/NL; 95 cl OPG/TR/S&T; 95 cr OPG/TR/NL; 95 b OPG/TR/RAD; 96 tl OPG/TR/S&T; 96 tr OPG/TR/20:21; 96 b OPG/TR/A; 97 tl OPG/TR/S&T; 97 tc OPG/TR/S&T; 97 tr OPG/TR/NL; 97 c OPG/TR/A; 97 b OPG/TR/NL; 98 t OPG/TR/NL; 98 c OPG/TR/TAR; 98 b OPG/TR/TAR; 99 t OPG/TR/NL; 99 c OPG/TR/TAR; 99 cr OPG/TR/NL; 99 bl OPG/TR/TAR; 99 bc OPG/TR/TAR; 99 br MILL/BC; 100 t OPG/TR/TAR; 100 b OPG/TR/TAR; 101 t OPG/TR/B; 101 c OPG/TR/A; 101 bl OPG/TR/TAR; 101 br OPG/TR/A/Persiflage; 102 tl OPG/TR/TAR; 102 tr OPG/TR/A/Christobal; 102 b OPG/TR/TAR; 103 tl OPG/TR/S&T; 103 tc OPG/TR/A/Christobal; 103 tr OPG/TR/A/Christobal; 103 b MILL/CSK; 104 t OPG/TR/RAD; 104 tr OPG/TR/MEM; 104 c OPG/TR/TAR; 104 b OPG/TR/NL; 105 t OPG/TR/RAD; 105 c t OPG/TR/RAD; 105 c b OPG/TR/RAD; 105 b OPG/TR/RAD; 106 tl OPG/TR/RAD; 106 tc OPG/TR/NL; 106 tp OPG/TR/NL; 106 b OPG/TR/NL; 107 tl OPG/TR/NL; 107 tr OPG/TR/NL; 107 b OPG/TR/NL; 108 t OPG/TR/TAR; 108 bl OPG/TR/TAR; 108 br OPG/TR/NL; 109 t OPG/TR/TAR; 109 c OPG/TR/TAR; 109 b OPG/TR/TAR; 110 HUL; 112 t OPG/TR/TAR; 112 c OPG/TR/TAR; 112 bl MILL/CHI; 112 br MILL/CHI; 113 t Patrick Rylands; 113 cl OPG/TR/A; 113 cr OPG/TR/B; 113 b OPG/TR/A; 114 tl MILL ; 114 tr OPG/TR/PB; 114 b MILL/CHI; 115 tl MILL/A/Collector's World; 115 tr OPG/TR/CHI; 115 b MILL; 116 t OPG/TR/A; 116 c OPG/TR/MEM; 116 b OPG/TR/A; 117 t OPG/TR/A; 117 c MILL; 117 b OPG/TR/A; 118 c OPG/IB/CSK; 118 b OPG/TR/A; 119 t OPG/TR/MEM; 119 cl MILL/BC; 119 cr MILL/BC; 119 b OPG/TR/MEM; 120 t OPG/TR/MEM; 120 c OPG/TR/MEM; 120 b OPG/TR/MEM; 121 tl OPG/TR/A; 121 tr OPG/TR/A; 121 b OPG/TR/MEM; 122 t OPG/TR/MEM; 122 c OPG/TR/MEM; 123 t OPG/TR/MEM; 123 bl OPG/TR/MEM; 123 br OPG/TR/MEM; 124 t OPG/TR/MEM; 124 c OPG/TR/MEM; 124 b OPG/TR/MEM; 125 t OPG/TR/MEM; 125 c MILL; 125 b OPG/TR/MEM; 126 tl Sotheby's London; 126 tr OPG/TR/MEM; 126 b OPG/TR/MEM; 127 t OPG/TR/MEM; 127 c OPG/TR/TAR; 127 b OPG/TR/MEM; 128 The Reel Poster Archive Company; 129 tl OPG/TR/MEM; 129 b The Reel Poster Archive Company; 130 t OPG/TR/MEM; 130 tc OPG/TR/MEM; 130 bl OPG/TR/NiG; 130 br MILL; 131 t MILL/Saffron Walden Saleroom; 131 c OPG/TR/TAR; 131 b The Reel Poster Archive Company; 132 t OPG/TR/NIG; 132 bl OPG/TR/NIG; 132 br OPG/TR/NIG; 133 t OPG/TR/NIG; 133 cl OPG/TR/; 133 cr OPG/TR/NIG; 133 b OPG/TR/NL; 134 t OPG/TR/DV; 134 bl OPG/TR/TAR; 135 tl OPG/TR/TAR; 135 tr OPG/TR/TAR; 135 bl OPG/TR/TAR; 135 br OPG/TR/B